"Christine and Jessica's *Innovating Play* could not have come at a better time. It's as though they predicted that educators across our country would need to engage with their students remotely. The Innovating Play Cycle is exactly what teachers need today to bring education alive to students who will learn differently in the future. Filled with practical insights and activities, *Innovating Play* needs to be in every primary teacher's hands."

—Dr. Jeff Wilson, superintendent, San Marino Unified School District, California

"*Innovating Play* reads so naturally because its authors speak from the heart. The ideas they share float directly from the pages and right into your classroom. The book is filled with a great mix of usable ideas and thoughtful reminders of how to infuse play into all classrooms. Pick up the book and start your playful partnership with Christine and Jessica today."

—Michael Matera, middle school teacher, speaker, and author of *Explore Like a Pirate*, Wisconsin

"*Innovating Play* is more than a creative collection of collaborative resources, it's about creating a culture of classroom community. Christine and Jessica make it very clear throughout the book how any elementary teacher can adapt the Innovating Play Cycle as a complement to his or her current teaching style. As a second grade teacher and avid Flipgrid and Seesaw educator, I was excited to see how the traditional methods presented in the book also easily translated into the user-friendly apps I know and love, like Google Drawings and Google Slides. *Innovating Play* is just the right piece of heartwork that will get elementary school teachers excited about all the possibilities of making it happen while creating lifelong learners along the way! May you discover excitement in the power of purposeful edtech and innovating play as you empower the voice and choice in each of your learners and find renewed joy in your own journey as you read this book and connect to the Innovating Play community."

—Adrienne Jimerson, second grade teacher, MAEd, KES TOY 2020–21, Virginia

"When you open *Innovating Play*, you are immersed in what early childhood teachers dream their classrooms could be. Christine and Jessica share not only their journey but all their resources so that you and your students can join them. It is the perfect balance of learning with hands-on and tech tools. A must-read for every early childhood educator that wants to deepen the learning of their students."

—Carol McLaughlin, primary teacher, Alabama

"Y'all, this book is a must-read for early childhood educators! Christine and Jessica have created a playbook of dynamic learning experiences for students. If you are looking for innovative teaching ideas that go beyond traditional thinking AND support social-emotional learning, this book has everything you need to get started."

—Kasey Bell, author of *Shake Up Learning*, blogger, podcaster, and digital-learning coach at ShakeUpLearning.com, Texas

"Jessica LaBar-Twomey and Christine Pinto have come up with an outstanding book that gives real-world examples and practical advice. *Innovating Play* should be added to the reading list for any teacher—new or veteran. Give it a try. Have some fun. You won't regret it."

—Rick Papera, superintendent,
New Jersey

"Christine and Jessica are two of the most skilled and passionate educators I have had the pleasure to connect with on Twitter. They have created a collaboration space (#InnovatingPlay) for teachers from around the world to connect virtually in that is both safe and challenging. The sense of community they have created for adults mirrors that which they have created for their kindergarten students, who likewise connect from across the country and time zones. This book has encouraged me to continue to take risks as an educator and build a strong community of learners in my own first grade classroom. *Innovating Play* serves as a guide for educators to create a safe and challenging classroom community that celebrates and PLAYS together!"

—Aubrey DiOrio, first grade teacher,
North Carolina

"*Innovating Play* provides guiding questions to help you reflect upon what you currently do in your own learning space. The book is full of developmentally appropriate ideas for helping students design and create with technology rather than just consuming it. Even though it's written by two kindergarten educators, this book is absolutely for *any* educator. The authors expertly weave technology, wonder, discovery, SEL, and balanced literacy into their Innovating Play Cycle, and their ideas will transform what you are doing with learning!"

—Courtney Stepp, kindergarten teacher,
Washington

"Connect, wonder, play, and discover your way through the examples and resources shared in *Innovating Play*. Imagine the possibilities for your students when they can collaborate outside the walls of your classroom, school, and district!"

—Scott Bramley, chief technology officer,
Arcadia Unified School District, California

"As a technology coach, I am always looking for original ideas to infuse interactive digital learning into a blended classroom. *Innovating Play* is filled with inspirational 'sticky' learning ideas! It shares examples of how typical lessons can be infused with a little technology to create even richer learning experiences that reach beyond the walls of your classroom. These are experiences that can easily be shared with students, families, communities, or even around the world! The ideas in *Innovating Play* are easily adaptable too! They have sparked my imagination with ways I can adapt or expand them for any grade level! If you're looking for a book that will inspire and excite you and is filled with resources, check out *Innovating Play*!"

—Michael Wesely, instructional technology specialist,
Virginia

Innovating Play

Innovating Play

Over 60+ Resources for Early Childhood Educators

Reimagining Learning through Meaningful Tech Integration

Jessica LaBar-Twomey and Christine Pinto

This book is available at special discounts when purchased in quantity for educational purposes or as premiums, promotions, or fundraisers. For inquiries and details, contact the publisher at books@daveburgessconsulting.com.

Published by Dave Burgess Consulting, Inc.
San Diego, CA
DaveBurgessConsulting.com

Library of Congress Control Number: 2020941685
Paperback ISBN: 978-1-951600-44-0
Ebook ISBN: 978-1-951600-45-7

Cover and interior design by Liz Schreiter

Editing and production by Reading List Editorial: readinglisteditorial.com

This book is dedicated to the educators who dream with action, the children who embrace limitless play, and the families who lovingly welcome the journey together. We are so grateful.

Contents

Introduction: Our Story

The idea for this book was born several summers ago, when the two of us—Jessica, a kindergarten teacher in New Jersey, and Christine, a kindergarten teacher in California—first met online. Up to that point we had followed one another on Twitter but hadn't found the time to really share our ideas in great detail. Christine was moderating the #GAfE4Littles #SlowFlipChat where Jessica was one of the participants.[1] We both liked connecting the Twitter handles of the fellow educators with whom we'd been interacting on Twitter to names and faces on Flipgrid. Educators who had only connected in 140 characters or less on Twitter came together via video on Flipgrid, and everyone's voice could be heard. We shared stories and united as colleagues with a common mindset and vision for children. Suddenly the world of teachers seemed smaller. Exploring new ways of learning and teaching felt limitless, and through that community we felt brave enough to expand our ideas and share them with others.

---

1 #SlowFlipChat is a slow-paced chat, or conversation, on Flipgrid or Twitter. In this particular chat, one question was posted each day for one week on both platforms. Educators who participated on Flipgrid recorded video responses to answer the questions and reply to others. Educators also had the choice to reply to the questions on Twitter in written form via Tweets.

It was also during that initial #SlowFlipChat when Jessica caught Christine's attention by the way she articulated her ideas about her classroom in her response videos. Her thoughts about design thinking and building empathy with her kindergartners while using technology were unique. Christine encouraged Jessica to start a blog, invited her to write a guest post on christinepinto.com, listened intently to what she had to say, and offered a gentle nudge forward when needed.

The following school year, we found opportunities for our classes to collaborate. Teaching in California, Christine posted an invitation to her class's Guess the Sharing Item Flipgrid on Twitter. Jessica saw the invitation, and her class jumped in and participated from New Jersey. Later on, Jessica posted an invitation to her class's Lego Creation Flipgrid on Twitter. Christine shared the Flipgrid with her students and had them share their Lego creations. Opportunities like these led us to wonder how our students could connect and collaborate on a more regular basis. A collaborative daily project (our weather reporting Flipgrid) emerged from that question. This collaboration occurred for the rest of the school year and surfaced special collaborative projects along the way.

As we arrived at another summer, a whole year after our initial interactions, we wondered about ways to streamline the connection between our classes. We knew that in order to delve deeper into our practice, we would need to develop a framework to follow. This would create the foundation for a collaboration that would provide meaningful daily experiences over the course of an entire year. We began by looking carefully at each of our schedules and curricular expectations, along with common goals and objectives, in order to weave together a cohesive collaboration between teachers and students. We knew that the collaboration could not be seen as "extra." We saw the potential to explore a new way of learning and teaching that would allow for a richer process and perspective while addressing the expectations each of us faced in our respective districts. Throughout the months of June, July, and August, we worked through every part of our daily teaching schedules together. When the next school year began, we were ready to put our ideas into action.

The Innovating Play Cycle

As educators our task is to tune into the needs and processes of the learners in our care. What inspires them? What challenges them? What can we do to reach them collectively and individually in order to support their growth and development? When we decided to explore the idea of Innovating Play by connecting our classrooms, we went from considering the needs of one class to considering the needs of a collective community of learners. It was important that our students eventually normalize the fact that they had a "New Jersey teacher" and a "California teacher."

Establishing this new norm meant paying particular attention to the patterns of learning and interactions that occurred. Although we used every resource we could find to support our educational decisions, we did not have a textbook or research to which we could specifically refer. Connecting classrooms of young children on opposite sides of the country on a daily basis for an entire year was brand-new territory in education. We knew when we started that we would be trailblazers, and that made us even more mindful of the pedagogical decisions we made.

In our first year of collaboration, we were particularly mindful of the flow of the interaction between our classes, and we started to notice patterns forming. Instead of deciding on projects and experiences ahead of time, we noted the reactions of our students to the opportunities for connection we had built. As we watched student interactions, we worked together as teachers to find the instances where we shared common curricular goals and objectives. We wanted to weave together intentional, productive, meaningful experiences. From this process a cycle began to emerge.

This cycle, which we call the Innovating Play Cycle, represents a pattern of play that students move through when engaging in a learning task or experience. While this cycle can take place as part of formal learning in the classroom, it is also an intuitive process that happens as people participate in informal learning and discovery. We have found that highlighting these elements of natural learning patterns within our lesson planning supports authentic engagement as students broaden and acquire depth of understanding. Planning, facilitating, and reflecting through the Innovating Play Cycle can enrich lesson-plan design across the curriculum.

Innovating Play Cycle

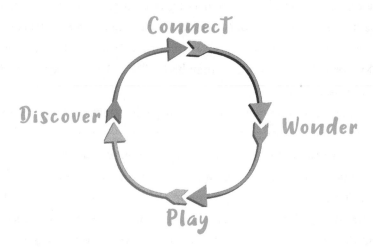

Connect: Every meaningful learning experience begins from a point of connection. Connection can come through just about any experience. In each chapter of this book we explain how a particular activity can become a connected one. You can take one of those ideas, or any learning experience you presently teach, and use technology to strengthen and further connections for children that reach beyond the classroom and into the world.

Wonder: When a connection inspires, it will naturally provoke wonder, or curiosity. The language of wondering is part of the culture of the early elementary classroom. Wondering comes in either the form of a statement (I wonder. . .) or a question. Lessons and experiences that begin with wonder hold authentic engagement opportunities. Lessons can also focus learners on questions that stir up curiosity about big ideas. We start with questions that begin with: What if. . . ? What happens when. . . ? Why. . . ? These higher-level questions give learners and teachers purpose as we prepare to deepen connection and understanding through the next phase of the cycle.

Play: What do we do with wonders? We play with them! Play comes in many forms: free and open-ended play, games, reading and writing, hands-on activities, and even exploration and creation through technology. We see every learning opportunity as a possible playground ready to be explored. In this part of the cycle, there is an important shift from a "traditional lesson" mindset to the mindset of playing with an idea or concept. Even simple vocabulary adjustments represent an important change in classroom culture (for example, replacing "The goal for today's lesson is. . ." with "Today we will play with the idea. . ."). Just as there is a language for wonder, there is a language for playful learning that contributes to the overall experience. In using words that reflect the importance of play, we empower children to see the role of learning as it applies to experiences that they naturally initiate as they seek to understand the world around them.

Discover: As the cycle reaches this culminating phase, we pause to consider the learning that has taken place. What new information has been uncovered? What misconceptions have been redefined? How can we share and move the learning that has taken place into the world beyond the classroom? Discovery is both reflective and active and moves us forward armed with new connections so that we can enter the Innovating Play Cycle once again.

Consider these questions when thinking about using the Innovating Play Cycle to explore and innovate when it comes to your classroom activities and lesson plans:

CONNECT

- Are there opportunities for learners and teachers to connect with each other within and beyond the classroom?
- Are there experiences that connect learning to the real world?
- Are there elements that move learning beyond the walls of the classroom in order to share and connect with families and expand the learning experience?

WONDER

- Are there opportunities for children and teachers to wonder together?
- Is there room for spontaneous wonder?
- Does the classroom culture and environment support a sense of wonder?
- What higher-level or big-picture questions can be asked to spark wonder?

PLAY

- Are there playful and joyful elements of learning incorporated into the classroom experiences?
- Are play-based experiences supportive of the level of academic learning that students need to obtain?
- Is there a shared, common vocabulary between teachers and students that creates a natural connection between learning and play?

DISCOVER

- Do the learning experiences provide opportunities for student discovery?
- Does the classroom culture provide a safe space for children to be able to communicate discoveries?
- Are there elements of instruction that allow discovery to move beyond the walls of the classroom?

Though in this book we focus on the possibilities for bringing our classes together to explore the Innovating Play Cycle, the cycle is in no way limited to classroom collaboration. It can be found within individual classrooms, across grade levels, between content areas, even beyond the classroom itself as authentic learning experiences emerge out in the world.

The Role of Technology and Empathy

What happens when we create a foundation for learning that includes technology as a shared human experience, beginning with our youngest students? We discover that we can build relationships that break down classroom walls and in the process learn how to communicate and collaborate on a deeper, more meaningful level.

In this book we connect the use of digital tools to the bigger picture of purposeful learning through play. When we begin with play, we follow children's natural instincts and support authentic learning connections. As we play we connect and share a common experience, and as a result of play we wonder about new ideas, explore new questions, and discover new interests. The cycle of play is essential to the emotional development of children and ought to be fully incorporated into their learning experiences. But how?

With today's technology, we can facilitate creative play that helps children make meaningful connections as an essential part of the classroom learning experience. We can start by asking questions like:

- What is happening beyond our classroom?
- What do schools look like for other children?
- How can we redesign rituals and routines to include a broader definition of the world?
- How do we create safe and beautiful multimedia spaces for children and teachers to connect daily? How can we use free and open-ended tools to create these experiences?

- How can we redefine the experiences we offer our learners so that they have a deeper, richer context for what it means to actively engage and participate in the world?
- How can we plan and discover together as teachers?
- How can we rethink what it means to be educated?

These are big questions, and while we are asking you to think about them, we are not leaving you alone to discover the answers. As classroom teachers, we have discovered so many possibilities (and continue to discover more!). We will share specific examples of our experiences with you and teach you how to create your own.

However, if there's one place to find an overarching "answer" in *Innovating Play*, it is in our embrace of a design-thinking approach to tech integration with a strong focus on developing empathy in students. In this thoughtful approach, teachers try to see from their students' perspectives in order to initiate meaningful and relevant experiences. To continue to nurture the growth of empathy, we focus on connecting students with their peers—both immediately in their classroom and on the other side of a screen—through these experiences. In this process, children improve their ability to put themselves in the shoes of others. By blending technology in education with a mindful approach, integrating it seamlessly rather than putting the tool at the forefront, we allow the students' experiences to take center stage.

It is the hearts and minds of children playing and learning together every day that will help us to redefine education and digital interaction in our current culture. From sharing daily routines and cultivating personal interactions to documenting rich experiences, technology offers us the tools that can bring students together from across the country and let their emotional development shine.

Before we send kids up the educational ladder to analyze sources, design solutions, communicate opinions and perspectives, and think critically about the world, we need to give them a language for empathy and the tools to safely interact in physical *and* virtual spaces. If we are going to nurture truly thoughtful human beings who can collaborate through technology, we need to build from the bottom up. We need to educate young children (and their families) by allowing them to imagine new possibilities and participate in learning together.

With this mindset we learn to stop teaching alone. We let go of the traditional limits of time and space and instead embrace the opportunity to reconceptualize students' classroom experience while supporting one another as educators. Most of all we empower all children to see their potential to shape and contribute to the world through joyful creation and a deep understanding of human connection beyond the screen.

Bringing Innovating Play to Your Learning Environment

Innovating Play was written with these goals in mind. It is designed to be an inspirational guide for teachers of young children who are passionate about the natural development of their students and interested in discovering how technology can help facilitate that process and expand their horizons. Inside, you'll find dozens of learning opportunities for classroom collaborations that lead to greater empathy, deeper understanding, and, most of all, a playful outlook.

The book is divided into four parts. Part One looks at three different rituals and routines that kick off the day in early elementary classrooms and explores how connecting through technology can deepen students' experiences and expand their ability to empathize. In Part Two we then turn to focus on early elementary curriculum in the areas of literacy, science, and mathematics to show how innovating play in the academic realm leads to joyful learners and a more comprehensive grasp of the material—all while fostering social-emotional development in students. In Part Three we investigate what happens when innovating play is "unchained" from traditional classroom expectations and students activate prior knowledge by exploring current learning concepts through Connected Play, foster connections across classrooms with Community Play, and even involve their families. Finally in Part Four we provide a rich trove of materials and resources for teachers who are ready to dive in and start experimenting with the Innovating Play Cycle.

Each chapter is designed in a similar fashion. We introduce the specific topic we are investigating in the chapter and explain its importance to students. We then show how using the Innovating Play Cycle approach can be transformed in the context of a collaborative classroom. Along the way we share anecdotes about particular experiences or examples to illustrate the impact of the Innovating Play approach and explore different directions teachers and students can take.

Each chapter is therefore an invitation to walk the path of Innovating Play with us. We will support you in developing a mindset that will potentially redefine your experience as an educator, your students' experience as learners, and those students' families' experiences as participants in the process of learning and teaching. As you consider the many learning opportunities presented in each chapter, we encourage you to see how the Innovating Play Cycle applies to your own students' experiences. We invite you to find new excitement, great joy, and endless possibilities in your process of learning and teaching through Innovating Play.

Bonus Resources

We've put together an abundance of online discussion questions, materials, and resources that build on what's in the book. These original Innovating Play resources may be shared, and copies of templates may be made in order for educators to customize experiences to meet the needs of their own students, families, and collaborating classrooms. All that we ask in return is that you acknowledge the role of Innovating Play in your process of learning and creating. One of our favorite things is when teachers share back with us! If you adapt or create an experience based on what is offered here, we welcome you to connect and share with the #InnovatingPlay Community on Twitter. We look forward to hearing from you and celebrating your journey through Innovating Play.

Innovating Play with Routines and Rituals

If you spend a day in a classroom in any subject or grade, you will see routines and rituals in full swing. Classrooms *thrive* on routine. Whether students are younger or older, kids naturally gravitate to patterns that repeat in order to begin the learning process. Young children in particular are just beginning to develop their understanding of how school works, and they require explicit direction and meaningful connection to routines to feel safe as learners and members of a classroom community.

Every classroom relies either explicitly or implicitly on the idea of routines and rituals to create a culture of learning. Typically these routines and rituals are limited to specific spaces and observations of what is close, immediate, and local, and are thus limited to the walls of the classroom itself. As a result, classrooms are treated as individual units, schools as separate buildings, districts as distinct entities, and states as discrete spaces for education. Yet the world is growing more interdependent, and the need to break down walls is more pressing than ever. With the development of technology, we are given the opportunity to reconsider these limits, forge deeper connections, and help our students learn more about the experiences of others and increase their capacity for empathy.

Designing Meaningful Rituals and Routines

When planning new experiences, it is important to first consider the overall purpose for learning and to break down the process of the experience from there. This backward design approach ensures that we stay true to our larger goals and intentions as educators. When innovating a ritual or routine, instead of starting by asking ourselves about the next technology experience we want to create, we must ask ourselves big-picture questions to tap into our intentions. For example, in the case of the Feelings Check-In (Chapter 2), we ask:

- What are the values and qualities of humanity that we want to nurture in learners?
- In what ways might a digital world require us to be more in tune with the feelings/emotions of ourselves and others?
- As educators, what are the essential questions we can ask our students when considering the feelings of others in both physical and virtual spaces?

From these questions we identified the need to know not only who is in our spaces, but what is happening with each person. We knew how we wanted to facilitate the discussion with the children; our next step was creating visuals that would support our conversation. That led us to asking ourselves more specific questions, much like the questions that we use when planning a lesson. These questions would not only support our creation, but would later guide us in finding depth in this routine for children throughout the year. The questions were:

- What if everyone felt the same?
- Why do we take time to recognize emotions in ourselves and others?
- How does the recognition of others' feelings in our shared space transfer to what we know about others beyond our spaces?
- How does having a shared digital space to explore emotions impact what we know about people we cannot otherwise see?

These questions not only serve as a guide to facilitate a ritual we carry out every day, but they also give us a check-in point with our design. If these are skills we want our children to acquire, then does our lesson design for the Feelings Check-In help them to answer these questions? In order to design meaningful rituals and routines, we need to stay focused on the larger purpose that we are trying to facilitate.

Through these routines and rituals, we embrace the use of technology to create foundational experiences for children's emotional development. These very first rituals promote a sense of safety and comfort.

As we introduce virtual spaces for connection via rituals and routines, we shift from the idea that children connect to their physical classroom space to the idea that tools can empower them to understand and self-regulate from anywhere. We offer them an opportunity to create shared experiences and thereby empathize with people beyond the walls of the classroom. We give them the tools in order to see, practice, and connect from anywhere. In that, we redefine what it means to be a learner in the classroom and beyond.

No matter which digital tools you select to facilitate your class experiences, we encourage you to consider the ways in which they help to support, define, develop, and tell the story of learning in your classroom and beyond. Here are some things to keep in mind as you make your selections:

- How does the tool allow you to impact relationships and build trust, acceptance, and understanding beyond your classroom?
- How does the tool allow you to support growth and learning because of the ways in which it connects people?
- How does the tool allow you to contribute to the development and/or communication of the story of learning?

A tool is just a platform with features and a canvas space. It is the creator who plays with the tool who generates meaning, magic, and possibilities.

Wish You Well

When establishing a classroom community, we consider a sense of safety, comfort, connection, and familiarity to be the most necessary components of rituals and routines. Children's first understanding of community is directly tied to their place in it; therefore, they need a space where they feel represented, accounted for, and recognized. A traditional approach to this routine would be some kind of roll call, allowing the teacher to recognize the students who are present and helping the children to understand which learners are sharing the classroom space on any given day.

As we redefine the limits of the classroom, we have the opportunity to redefine this routine and expand our students' sense of the space they share. In rethinking this routine we want to grow and develop the capacity of children to flow between "the world I see" and "the world beyond me." This is a particularly big reach for young children who are in a developmentally egocentric stage. To help them grow we can use these gentle rituals and routines to begin to scaffold a more expansive understanding of the self and develop their sense of empathy.

If intentionally designed, these routines and rituals can guide children toward asking and answering questions that revolve around the ideas of "How can we tell what is happening in the classroom?" and "How do we know what is happening with others outside our classroom?"

Transforming the Wish You Well Ritual

As children settle into the classroom, they are welcomed with a variety of hands-on learning experiences. We value balanced, independent, active, playful engagement to start the day. This time is meant to activate prior knowledge while exposing learners to a variety of materials, processes, and tools. Children know this time as Connected Play, which will be addressed in detail later in the book in Chapter 7. As this time comes to a close, children are gently signaled to clean up and assemble in the community gathering space. Students shift from focusing on independent and small-group collaboration to understanding their role within the larger classroom community. During our community gathering time, we engage in a series of rituals in order to support children's understanding of the ways in which their participation and engagement in the larger group impact the collective experience. In this chapter we break down the Wish You Well ritual so that we can clearly demonstrate the ways in which we guide students to establish a unique perspective of the learning community as a whole.

Innovating Play Bonus Resources:
Find more at consciousdiscipline.com

We adopted the Wish You Well ritual from the social-emotional learning program Conscious Discipline to acknowledge children who are absent from school that day. A poster of a heart with children's names and/or faces arranged around the heart is shown to students. Anyone who is absent is placed inside the heart. Everyone then places their hands on their heart and lightly taps their chest while singing the "Wish You Well" song (sung to the tune of "The Farmer in the Dell"):

We wish you well.
We wish you well.
All through the day today,
we wish you well!

When we first considered exploring the idea of connecting classes daily, it made sense to consider routines that were already in place for each of us. Christine had already been using the Wish You Well Heart, and so sharing this routine seemed a natural way to create a connection between our classes and establish a safe space for all of our children. In order to develop a joint Wish You Well Heart, we used the virtual tool Google Drawing and gave each other editing permissions so that both classes would have access.

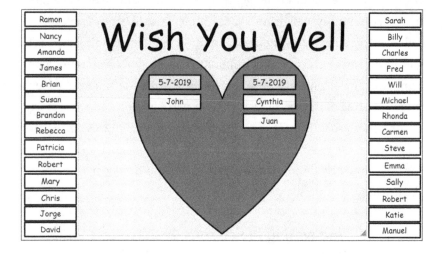

Through our shared Wish You Well Heart, both classes could learn the names of all the children and have a sense of who was present and absent in the other classroom. The time difference meant that the New Jersey Wish You Well check-in happened well before the kids in California had gotten to school, so it became part of the daily routine in New Jersey to see which children had been present the day before in California. The students in California, on the other hand, learned who was currently present in New Jersey during their check-in.

Innovating Play Bonus Resources:
Find more at innovatingplay.world/wishyouwell

Many observations take place during these check-ins which help students develop the ability to notice details about—and even trigger a deeper awareness of—what may be happening in their friends' school day. For example, as part of the routine in California, students change the date in the Wish You Well Heart and cross-check to see if it matches the date in New Jersey. If it does, we know the New Jersey class got to the ritual that day. If not, the children have learned to understand that their New Jersey counterparts' morning was different in ways that are impossible for us in California (e.g., snow day) or in ways that are relatable (e.g., having an assembly first thing in the morning).

Through this ritual, both classes broadened their sense of community while developing a sense of safety and comfort. They started to naturally consider both what was close and observable and the world outside what they could immediately see. Through the Wish You Well ritual, seeds of wonder were planted as children asked questions about the absent students, such as:

- Why are they absent?
- How many days have they been gone?
- Are they sick?
- Are they on vacation?
- How can we let them know we are thinking of them?

From 2,500 miles away this small routine nurtured a sense of caring and empathy that was real and prompted us to look for actions we could take to answer these questions.

Faciliation Questions for the Wish You Well

TRADITIONAL WITH A POSTER

- Who is absent from class today?
- What clues can we look for to find his/her name or picture to place in the Wish You Well Heart?
- Do we have any information about why our friend is not in class?
- Why is it important to recognize our classmates who are not here and send well-wishes to friends?

ENHANCED BY GOOGLE DRAWING

- Where are the numbers on the keyboard to change the date on our Wish You Well Heart? Will today's number come before or after yesterday's number?
- Which name do we need to click to move into the Wish You Well Heart? How do we know which one it is?
- How do we move an object or text box on the screen? How do we know that the object or text box is ready to move? What happens on the screen?

TRANSFORMED BY COLLABORATING WITH ANOTHER CLASS

- How many friends are absent from our class today? How many friends are absent from our friends' class? How many friends are absent from kindergarten altogether?
- Which class has more friends absent today?
- What do we know about the friends who are absent in our class? Do we have any information about the friends in the other class?
- Why is it important to send well-wishes to friends near and far? How does this connect to other family members and friends you know?
- The Wish You Well Heart is a shared digital space. Should we ever move names on their side of the heart? Why not?
- Why is it important to be respectful in a shared digital space?

Sonya's Story

At one point, Christine shared with Jessica that one of her students, Sonya, would be out of school for a period of time due to illness. Jessica took this as an opportunity for her class to extend the Wish You Well experience and transfer the ritual to a real-life context. When facilitating the Wish You Well routine the following day, Jessica let her students know that their classmate in California, Sonya, was sick and would be out of school longer than usual. She posed questions to the children like "What do we do for someone who is not feeling well? How do we extend well-wishes beyond our Wish You Well Heart?" Children made connections to what they would do for family members and their immediate friends in the same situation. They suggested cards, texts, and even Kmail (i.e., Google Slides shared between the classes; more about Kmail in Chapter 4). Jessica then drew their attention to the tools that they used every day to communicate with classmates across the country. "Would it be possible for us to sing Sonya the 'Wish You Well Song' and share it with her? What tools could we use to share with her right now?" The children quickly identified the possibility of using our shared Seesaw class (a digital space in which students in both classes are connected to each other and their families; learn more about a shared Seesaw class in Chapter 8).[1] Together the students in New Jersey used the video tool in Seesaw to sing to Sonya. Later that day they were thrilled to hear Sonya's recorded response, in which her joyful tone clearly showed that their message and intentions had been received. This real-life example illustrates just one of the many ways in which simple routines and rituals can plant seeds of wonder and action that empower children to empathize with others in both physical and virtual spaces.

Bringing the Ritual into Student Play

One of the clearest indicators that a child has understood and internalized an experience is when they transfer that understanding beyond

---

1   Seesaw is a digital platform for student portfolios and parent communication.

the original context of the lesson. We see this happen when children return to books we have enjoyed together and reenact scenarios, role-play, and pretend.

In our classrooms, digital spaces provide playgrounds for children to re-create experiences as well. During Community Play (learn more about Community Play in Chapter 8), Chromebooks and iPads are available to children to facilitate a variety of experiences throughout the classroom. These digital tools provide teachers a window into the minds of learners as they make choices about how to use the technology and blend it into their play.

On one particular afternoon, Jessica noticed one of her students, Michael, looking at the Wish You Well Heart hanging in the classroom, after which he requested a Chromebook. "Is it OK if I make my own Wish You Well Heart?" he asked. "I think I can make it in [Google] Slides." They talked through the necessary steps he would need to take, including the use of shapes, color, Word Art, and text features in the Google Slides menu. Once a plan was in place, Jessica stepped back and carefully observed how Michael developed his own Wish You Well Heart. He thoughtfully and patiently manipulated the tools, he included his classmates' names by looking at resources around the classroom, and he added the name of his buddy in California (the buddy system is explained in Chapter 8). It was not long before other children saw what Michael was doing and began to teach each other how to make and personalize their own versions of the Wish You Well Heart.

Jessica snapped a photo of Michael with his Wish You Well Heart on his Chromebook so he could share it in the shared Seesaw class with his buddy in California.[2] He drew an arrow to his buddy's name and recorded a voice message stating that he'd put him in his Wish You Well Heart. His buddy in California smiled upon seeing Michael's Seesaw post and learning that he had been included in Michael's creation. He left Michael a voice comment saying "thank you." Other students in Christine's class also saw Michael's post in the shared Seesaw class, and the experience inspired some of them to begin making their own Wish You Well Hearts.

In each classroom, children developed ways in which they could re-create the shared ritual and also carefully recognize the people that were important to them. Through this experience, they learned digital citizenship, not as a formal lesson provided by the teacher, but as an authentic discovery that happened through play. The kid-created Wish You Well Hearts became living documents that empowered the children to see their creative potential through technology and use it to express positive thoughts to people near and far. It is discoveries like these that begin to solidify their understanding that, in both face-to-face and digital spaces, words and actions matter.

---

2   If your school allows the sharing of Google Docs with users outside of your district's domain, another option is simply locating the share button and typing in the email address of the recipient.

Connecting Literacy to the Ritual

In Chapter 4 we will explore the myriad of possibilities for connecting social-emotional development to literacy learning. However, literacy connections do not have to be limited to literacy instruction time. For example, when placing children's names in the heart, we take the opportunity to teach by using their names. For instance, if Sarah is absent, we will make the "s" sound and then ask students what letter they need to look for to find the absent student's name. If you decide to implement this ritual, we can guarantee that you will come up with your own teachable moments.

When developing rules and routines in the classroom, we look for every opportunity to connect academic concepts in meaningful ways. For example, since the virtual Wish You Well was created in Google Drawing, we were able to easily transfer it to a printable template in Google Slides, allowing us to extend the experience and create our own Wish You Well class books. On each page we provided a space for the child to write his or her name and an empty heart where he or she could draw a self-portrait.

The simple repetitive pattern of the "Wish You Well" song makes it ideal for emergent readers, while adding their names to the book helps the children create a personal connection to letters and words. Compiling all of these pages produced a simple and meaningful class book that reinforced their contribution to and understanding of community.

When children link academic concepts to comforting rituals, they make an emotional connection to their learning that can create a deeper foundation for them moving forward. Children repeatedly returned to the book when visiting the classroom library, pointing to the words to sing the song and read their friends' names with pride. It made the Wish You Well ritual even more meaningful for everyone involved.

Extended Learning Experience with Families

As we innovate routines and rituals to support connected classrooms, families should be included in these connections. This can be achieved through communication tools like Seesaw, where learning experiences can be accessed and shared at home by families. For instance, the Wish You Well book can be shared with families by turning it into an Adobe Spark Video.[3] Take pictures of each page from the Wish You Well book, insert them into Adobe Spark, select your preferred music, and the video is complete! As a bonus you can record the class singing the "Wish You Well" song and include that so it plays on the page with the lyrics.

Innovating Play Bonus Resources:
Find more at innovatingplay.world/wywclassbook

Throughout this book we will share a number of reflective questions. We see the value for educators in not only taking the time to reflect individually but also connecting with other educators to hear their reflections, discoveries, and ideas. To create this discussion

---

3   Adobe Spark Video is an online video-making tool that enables the integration of images, videos, music, and audio recordings.

opportunity, we have posted some reflection questions on Twitter and invited the Innovating Play Community to contribute their thoughts and ideas. This allows *you* to reflect and join the discussion by sharing your response on Twitter as well.

Learning with the #InnovatingPlay Community

Share a routine or ritual that you use to promote a sense of belonging and community within your classroom. Consider ways that this can also translate to alternative learning spaces.

innovatingplay.world/bookq1

Feelings Check-In

The Wish You Well ritual quickly presented us with our first connection point in a daily collaboration between classes. We recognized the ways this ritual helped us to expand the feeling of community both within and between our classrooms. Since we already knew who was in our spaces based on the Wish You Well, we began to wonder how we could acknowledge the energy in the room based on how the children were feeling. This would require some type of "check-in" with them.

It is important to note that the Innovating Play Cycle can happen both between students engaged in experiences and between collaborating teachers who carefully build and develop experiences together. In the case of the Wish You Well ritual, we as teachers moved deeper into the Wonder part of the Innovating Play Cycle as we brainstormed conventional approaches to checking in with our students, such as sharing in a circle, using hand signals to respond to prompts, and peer-to-peer check-in. On their own, these traditional classroom routines possess many of the values that we would want to uphold at any point in time. However, this was also our opportunity to reach deeper into our innovative mindset as we asked ourselves:

- How can we offer children a variety of self-reflection and self-regulation tools that they can return to at any point?

- How can we support the development of a richer vocabulary for communicating a variety of feelings and emotions?
- How can we actively engage children in practicing and applying emotional skills and strategies?
- What tools do we have at our disposal that we can bring into a shared space?
- How can we create an experience that is available to all children anywhere in the world?
- How can we empower families to follow up and use strategies for emotional development at home?

We saw the opportunity to empower children to develop their ability to identify their own emotions and read the facial cues and body language of their peers around them. Identifying your own emotion is one thing; knowing how to react to or support someone else with an emotion—whether to embrace it or feel it and move on—is another. With this in mind, we saw the potential to nurture our students' understanding that all human beings, both children and adults, experience the same range of emotions no matter where they are in the world. We saw this as an opportunity to create a common ground between our classes where we could shift into the Play part of our cycle to explore these ideas together. We embraced the idea of a digital creation that would enable students in both classes to acknowledge what it is for each

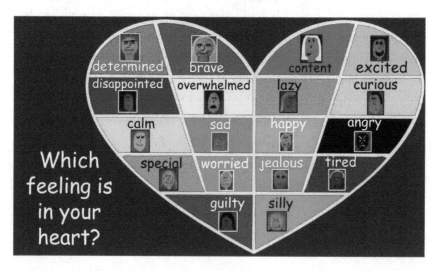

of us to be a person with feelings and unique experiences. We recognized the need to create a playful outlet that would be a safe space to explore and participate in self-reflection and self-regulation, *and* to express caring and empathy.

With these ideas in mind, the Feelings Check-In was born.

Transforming the Feelings Check-In

We begin this experience by doing a "teacher check-in" first, where the teacher quietly looks into the eyes of every child and reads the facial cues and body language of the children. It means a lot to the children when their feelings are acknowledged, even with silent recognition of a facial response back from their teacher. For example, if a child has a sad expression, the teacher can respond with gentle eye contact and a nod. On the contrary, if a child looks happy, the teacher can respond with a smile.

Innovating Play Bonus Resources:
Find more at innovatingplay.world/feelingsheart

Next, children are invited to silently check in with each other, looking around the room at their peers' facial cues and body language to identify emotions. The teacher then guides a discussion in order to help the children articulate their observations; he or she may ask, "What did you notice about a friend around you? How did you know how that friend is feeling? What were the specific clues that helped you to know?" Children then take turns sharing their observations, and corresponding children are invited to say if the observation matches how they are actually feeling and why.

Conversations like these give children opportunities to share, feel validated, and connect with the experiences and feelings of others. Some conversations open up possibilities for discussions about why a person's expression may not match exactly how he or she is feeling. Recognizing that people may sometimes hold a feeling in, unintentionally have an expression that does not match their feeling, or simply be misinterpreted are important life skills. All of these rich discussion opportunities allow for deeper connections within the classroom.

Children become more aware of others throughout the day as they learn, play, and problem-solve in various situations. Their vocabulary grows as they learn to articulate in complete sentences, ask questions, describe observations, and communicate their experiences. This simple practice creates a stronger sense of community that is essential for successful learning.

In the next part of the Feelings Check-In, we turn our students' attention to the Feelings Heart slide. A child is invited to select either a feeling to address a personal emotion or something he or she has noticed that a classmate needs. The heart contains drawings of feelings and the names of them. Each feeling in the heart is linked to its own slide, which has a selection of videos from GoNoodle meant to address that feeling.[1]

On each feeling slide, we use train engine visuals to support the children's understanding of the feeling and how it may impact our learning. The goal is to support children in recognizing the ways in which addressing our feelings helps to keep our trains on the track as learners. Certain feelings make us feel slow, which can make learning hard. In that case, we select a video that might help us to find energy as learners. Some feelings make us feel like we're going too fast and careening out of control, which makes it hard to enjoy and be productive in our learning. In this case, we might choose a more calming video to address the feeling.

Innovating Play Bonus Resources:
Find more at innovatingplay.world/engines

---

1   GoNoodle is a digital tool that has a range of child-appropriate movement and mindfulness videos.

After selecting the feeling and the complementary GoNoodle video to address the feeling, children return to the Feelings Heart for the last step in the check-in process. This is the point at which we take a moment to recognize that we can value every feeling. We allow children to see that human beings have the power to feel and to embrace what we feel. We help them to know that recognizing feelings supports us as learners and as members of our physical and virtual classroom communities. To bring closure to the experience we click on the gratitude slide and take a moment to acknowledge the ways in which we are lucky to be learning and playing in our classroom and with friends beyond our physical space.

We use the same Feelings Check-In slides in both of our classrooms, which generates another space we share digitally. By choosing to share spaces that are focused on feelings, we are letting the kids know that feelings are important. Shared digital spaces that value emotional connections create opportunities for children to understand that beyond the screen there are other human beings.

While this experience was facilitated in each of our classrooms individually, it was the collaboration through the Innovating Play Cycle that led to the creation, transformation, and facilitation of a common experience for both classes. As we developed the relationship between our collaborating classes, we discovered that not all experiences require children and teachers to be directly engaged with the other class; the creation of experiences that build a shared culture between classes is equally important. When teachers transform and implement new practices together, this becomes part of the shared culture. Mutual vocabularies, belief systems, and values allow for an increased depth of understanding throughout the collaboration between classes. Spending time creating rich experiences that contribute to the foundation of the learning community as a whole can lead to a more fulfilling overall experience for teachers and students alike.

On any given day, children in New Jersey and California will be choosing from the feelings depicted on the same Feelings Heart, which means those feelings must be experienced in both spaces. The Feelings Check-In addresses self-reflection, empathy between people in a shared physical space, and empathy for others beyond the classroom. It is this deep understanding that can potentially transfer to every other digital interaction that children have for the rest of their lives.

If we begin with the foundation of technology as a shared human experience, we break down barriers, build solutions, lift each other up, create possibilities for living, and elevate humanity.

Facilitation Questions for the Feelings Check-In

TRADITIONAL WITH OR WITHOUT A FEELINGS CHART

- What word could you use to describe how you are feeling today? Why?
- What do you notice about how a friend is feeling? How do you know?
- What questions can you ask your friend to see if your observations match his or her feelings?
- What can we do when we have that feeling?
- Does that emotion help you as a learner or does it make your job harder?

ENHANCED BY GOOGLE SLIDES

- Would you like to share how you are feeling or take care of a friend when you choose a feeling to explore today?
- Why are you feeling that way or why would you like to take care of that friend?
- What do you notice about the train(s) that match that feeling? What does that tell us about having this feeling as a learner?
- Which strategy will you choose so we can work on that feeling together?
- Why do we end our Feelings Check-In with gratitude?
- What can you share about your gratitude today?

TRANSFORMED BY COLLABORATING WITH ANOTHER CLASS

- If our buddy class is working on the Feelings Check-In as well, what does this help us to know about the feelings of people anywhere?
- Based on what we know from the Wish You Well Heart (or other recent collaborative experiences), what feelings might our buddies explore today? Why?
- Why is it important to understand that all people have feelings even when we cannot see them in the same space?

Extended Anecdote

As we developed the experience of the Feelings Check-In, one of our many challenges was to try and create an experience that is available to all children anywhere in the world. In March 2020, teachers across the United States began asking a very similar question as it applied to learning in general. Due to quarantine regulations to stop the spread of COVID-19, remote learning became a quick reality for many schools around the world. Right away, we recognized how the learning experiences that we had created through our collaboration would serve our students and their families in ways beyond what we had previously imagined. One of the very first things we transferred to our remote learning spaces was access to the Feelings Check-In. We each created a new grid for video responses in Flipgrid where the Feelings Check-In became our first focus topic. Children would be able to access the published link to the Feelings Heart and connect with each other in video format via Flipgrid. We knew that before children could feel safe as learners in an at-home setting, they would need a space to identify and share feelings, see and respond to each other, and find gratitude every day as they engaged in a completely new learning format. As they shared each day, we were able to nurture them individually by responding to each one on Flipgrid. We validated feelings and offered comfort. We reminded them of the tools they had available to help work through their feelings so we could continue our learning together. We listened to their moments of gratitude for big things such as friends, family, and teachers. As time went on, we recognized the ways that their new reality also shifted where they found their gratitude. Children shared that they were grateful for birthdays, glow sticks, flowering trees, bikes, walks outside, wind chimes, dream catchers, and gardens. They settled into the new version of a familiar routine and reflected back to us the ways that our vision of connected classrooms had formed a foundation deeper than we had anticipated at its conception.

Peace Corner

When offering rituals to support social-emotional growth and development, we try to ensure that we include opportunities for authentic application that carry over within and beyond the classroom. As we developed the Feelings Check-In, we knew that to be most effective, it would also need a place that was accessible to children throughout the day, as well as to families at home. In our classrooms we have a dedicated space called the Peace Corner to support children in identifying, self-soothing, and refocusing emotions so that they can productively engage in learning and interacting in the classroom.

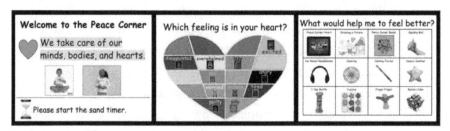

Innovating Play Bonus Resources:
Find more at innovatingplay.world/peacecorner

This space is located in a quiet corner of the classroom where children are provided a five-minute sand timer, visual reminders, and a variety of sensory materials from which they can select when they need emotional release or grounding. In this space a special version of the Feelings Heart is available on a classroom device for children to use independently as one of the focus options. Routines for the Peace Corner are introduced at the beginning of the year through the use of specific modeling (such as treating materials gently and with respect) and a class anchor chart, which is a visual model that breaks down each step. We created our anchor charts in Google Slides to offer students a visual resource to process and organize their ideas. Our anchor chart template provides three sections to support students' understanding of routines and rituals that may occur in the classroom throughout the day; placing these columns side by side highlights the need for all members of the classroom community to be fulfilling different roles at the same time. The leftmost section of the chart breaks down the role of the teacher in a given experience. By articulating the teacher-focus, children have a clear expectation of what he or she will be doing during this time. The middle section of the chart focuses on the role of the students during this time. Visual images help emergent readers to understand their responsibilities and foster independence and accountability. The last section of the chart is created collectively by the students and

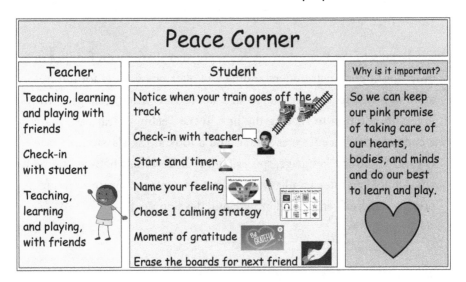

teachers so they can clearly demonstrate their understanding of why the process of this routine is important for the experience as a whole. (Anchor chart resources are included in Chapter 11.)

Extended Learning Experience with Families

As teachers we have the privilege of guiding not only the students that enter the classroom each day but also the families and caretakers who are connected as part of our learning community. Once the routine for the Feelings Check-In has been developed, the published link to the Feelings Heart can easily be shared with families via email or a family communication app so that they can use it as a tool for emotional expression and development at home. As teachers and families work together to problem-solve and help children process and articulate feelings, the Feelings Heart becomes a safe space for opening up and starting a conversation.

Innovating Play Bonus Resources:
Find more at innovatingplay.world/pcresource

Details of the Peace Corner setup are also shared with families in order to support their understanding and offer possibilities for the creation of a safe space for children to practice navigating feelings in the home. In addition to sharing the link to the Feelings Heart, we share a copy of our Peace Corner visuals and a look at the classroom Peace Corner. Common language, spaces, and even materials between home and school can offer families and educators common ground for supporting children's emotional growth and development.

One of Jessica's families shared the following about the Peace Corner they created at home with their son:

> Here is his Peace Corner we did this weekend. I gave him a bin, and we put things in it he can use. He is holding the sequined sloth that he loves. He also picked the color blue for the light behind him. He used it once this weekend!

Learning with the #InnovatingPlay Community

What are some self-reflection and self-regulation tools around feelings that you offer your students? What resources support you with social-emotional learning?

innovatingplay.world/bookq2

Morning Message

When students enter the classroom they come to expect a predictable collective opening experience once they have settled into the space. As young learners, children develop a fundamental understanding of how school works through the routines and expectations that are provided. Just as the Wish You Well and Feelings Check-In bring children together to promote a sense of order and connection, the Morning Message provides the opportunity to deepen the sense of community, clarify events of the day, introduce or revisit concepts, and provide instructional opportunities for concepts, skills, and strategies. Although the Morning Message formats may differ between classrooms, the underlying intention is largely the same: It is a literacy-based experience meant to bring learners together in order to support social, emotional, and academic growth using a simple and straightforward written-letter format for guidance and instruction.

As with all of the routines and rituals we present in this book, we never advocate getting rid of what is already best practice in your work. Rather, it is our intention to plant seeds for new ideas, provide examples and opportunities for growth, and spark inspiration to rethink those routines. Even best practices are in constant need of reevaluation. As the world changes, so must the experiences that we provide our children. To ignore shifts in the workings of the larger world is to miss an opportunity to reimagine possibilities in the classroom. To miss an opportunity is to miss the chance to make our work richer, deeper, more joyful, and more engaging for teachers and children.

Innovating Play Bonus Resources: Find more at responsiveclassroom.org/good-morning-learners

With that, we invite you into our Morning Message routine in order to begin to create or redefine your own Morning Message experiences. Whether you take baby steps through the SAMR model described later in this chapter or jump right in and start changing things up, our hope is that redefining the Morning Message will bring new imagination, excitement, and discovery into your classroom.

Transforming the Morning Message Ritual

The Morning Message is often the first point of connection for new learning focuses and experiences as we begin days and weeks with our classes. It is here that we plant the seeds for what is to come, as well as set up daily space for moving instruction forward. Including focus questions, skills, and strategies (all of which will be explored in the Extended Reading section of Chapter 4) can help to build a rich Morning Message experience. When developing Morning Messages, we also encourage you to consider the ways in which you can use your Google Slides deck to create an efficient workflow of instruction throughout your literacy block. Adding additional slides (containing focus questions, interactive games, images, or videos) after each Morning Message to facilitate Extended Reading experiences can allow for easy access and organization and help to maximize learning time and efficiency in the classroom.

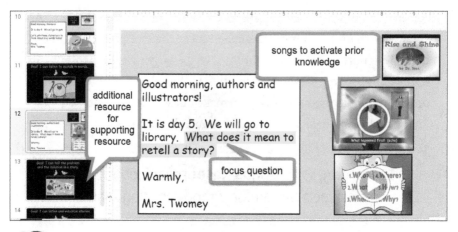

Innovating Play Bonus Resources: Find more at innovatingplay.world/messageinspiration

The Morning Message is not only a predictable routine, it is a place to reengage students or introduce them to new experiences or academic concepts. When creating a Morning Message, we have the opportunity to implement exciting and engaging anticipatory sets by connecting songs/videos, organizing a game, setting up a brainstorming space, or asking a big-picture question for discussion based on the skills we are practicing. Creating a meaningful Morning Message means setting it up as a space from which all other learning pieces can grow. We have found that the practice of planning out the ELA block of experiences for the week creates a guideline for Morning Message focuses. Once the week is planned, we are able to see where we would like to guide the children's attention each day, and we can create a balance of corresponding experiences throughout the week. Furthermore, working in Google Slides (as opposed to writing on a whiteboard or chart paper, for example) means that Morning Messages can be created from anywhere and prepared ahead of time. This enables teachers to use their planning and preparation time more efficiently.

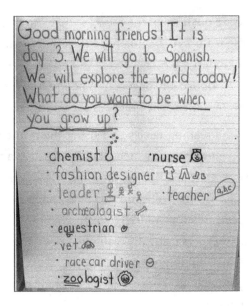

In Jessica's classroom the Morning Message has always been a special part of the kindergarten day. Even on traditional chart paper the children joyfully participated in the shared experience as they:

- Found comfort and security in knowing what would be happening in their school day
- Recognized what it feels like to be a reader
- Embraced opportunities to teach their peers and lead the class
- Experienced a sense of connection as they recognized their own growth and the growth of their peers
- Took their turn to select a favorite smelly marker and display their thinking on the message paper
- Discovered ways to show respect for all learners as they recognized what the process involved from both the teacher and learner perspectives
- Demonstrated learning transfer, as they would return to the message during free time to "play school" with their peers

As we prepare to redefine the Morning Message experience, take the time to list the qualities of your current Morning Message which hold the most value. Which pieces of the experience do you want to protect? Why are they important?

Just as there are qualities of the message that you will want to protect, there are also features of facilitation that teachers will want to consider. In Jessica's kindergarten, there were several practices to which the children clearly responded and engaged. When rethinking the Morning Message, these were some of the practices she considered:

- Waking the reading fairies and using them to track text (i.e., shaking a glitter wand, which would be used as a pointer)
- The use of echo reading to promote a safe emergent literacy experience in which all children could feel like readers
- The opportunity for children to be teachers and show what they noticed as readers using the reading fairies or smelly markers to indicate their thinking
- The experience of choosing to be a "reader" or a "leader" in front of peers
- The opportunity to set a reading goal and receive feedback from peers

Take time to identify the features of Morning Message facilitation that you find most valuable. What is it about these practices that makes them effective and engaging?

With these valued qualities and practices in mind, it's time to imagine possibilities! When we began exploring options for the Morning Message, we kept Dr. Ruben Puentedura's SAMR model in mind.[1] We recognized that any step on the path toward innovating is a step forward. As we break down this model, you can refer to the "SAMR for Morning Message in Google Slides" image ahead.

Even beginning with a simple substitution like writing your Morning Message in Google Slides will have surprise advantages that you may not have considered. When Jessica first switched to Google Slides to write the Morning Message, one thing she quickly realized was that making a mistake did not mean rewriting a whole new message on a new piece of chart paper! Details like this matter in teacher workflow and efficiency. The fact that a Morning Message in Google Slides

---

1 Details of Dr. Puentedura's SAMR model can be found at his website: http://hippasus.com/blog/.

is easily edited, saved, and available to revisit anytime makes the simple substitution an immediate win.

Looking more closely at how we could enhance the Morning Message experience by moving it to Google Slides, we noted the text feature tools that would allow children to demonstrate their thinking in new ways. Options such as highlighting, bolding, italicizing, underlining, and changing font and letter sizing would expose children to new ways of exploring text. The opportunity to work with text features that would imitate the look of a real book adds a new element for emergent readers that is not available through traditional chart paper. Using this format would also provide authentic instructional opportunities for working within Google Slides. Repeated daily exposure to these techniques gives children the chance to solidify their understanding of how to work within this digital space, which opens up options for individual learning, whole-class collaborative learning, and future creation opportunities. Much of the children's comfort with technology that you will see represented in this book stems directly from exposure and modeling through the Morning Message.

As we continued to modify the vision for creating learning opportunities within the Morning Message, we noted the ways that we could move beyond the limited use of text in order to include other multimedia formats and create a richer literacy experience. The addition of photos and images, videos, music, and audio features enhances the experience for learners by broadening the resources from which they can learn. With the inclusion of these elements, the message comes to represent a more comprehensive view of literacy.

Innovating Play Bonus Resources: Find more at innovatingplay.world/customizemaster

Finally, we looked at this new version of the message as a whole and saw the ways it now represented a learning experience that could shift beyond and between classrooms. As collaborating teachers, we would be able to build messages together, setting the stage for the common language that would be needed for project collaboration between classes. The message could also be shared with families for follow-up at home, as well as with teachers who might be working with individual

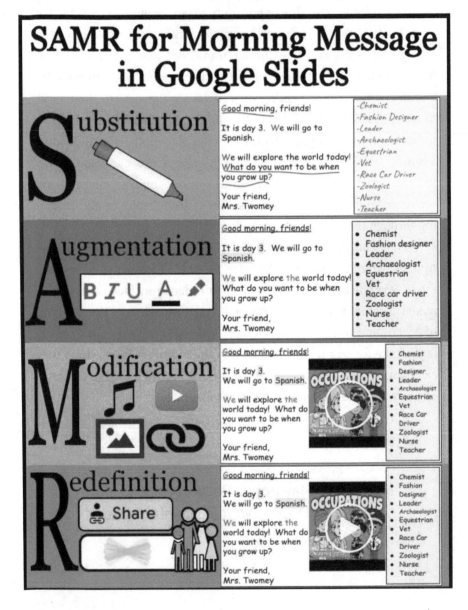

students and providing different types of instructional support during the day. A Morning Message that can live beyond the walls of the classroom and facilitate connection in multiple ways while representing a comprehensive view of literacy as it exists in the world is evidence of its full redefinition as an instructional resource and experience for children.

Creating a Space for Magic and Protecting the Fairies

To create safe and inspiring learning experiences for children and build their confidence and joy, we use a variety of special tools in the classroom to draw their attention to print. Of all these tools, the reading fairies are the children's absolute favorite. These are simply wands (available on Amazon) with liquid and glitter or confetti inside that moves when gently shaken.

"Waking the fairies" means that a child gets to shake a wand to make the glitter swirl. We gently wake the fairies so that they are ready to see every single word that we point to and read. We wake them every day for shared reading experiences with big books, as part of read-the-room experiences, and even across content areas such as math or science when we use the fairies to track numbers while counting or to point out details of a science investigation. Before all of that, however, we always wake them for Morning Message. So, as we transformed the Morning Message ritual, we knew that keeping a space to wake the reading fairies at the beginning of the Morning Message was absolutely non-negotiable!

Innovating Play Bonus Resources:
Find more at innovatingplay.world/fairies

If we were going to protect this ritual, we asked ourselves how we could make it even better. Adding videos to Google Slides turns the Morning Message into an auditory and visual experience. When developing the message slides, we created master slide layouts in order to make writing the daily Morning Message faster and easier. Jessica's master slide includes a space for the video of Dr. Jean's "Rise and Shine" song, which quickly became known as the song to "wake the fairies." Being able to start the song directly from the slide means that there aren't any outside tools to manipulate, and the children can immediately start singing along. What was once a simple, happy routine became even more special as we added music and video to enhance the experience.

One of the most engaging elements of the Morning Message for children is the way in which they can share the pen and participate in the experience. Although there is certainly value in continuing to offer children the opportunity to work with writing instruments and paper to show their thinking (and kids will always love those smelly markers!), using slides for Morning Message opens up new possibilities for children to demonstrate and visualize their thinking. We also open up opportunities to model and empower children to use tools in Google Slides that will be a part of other experiences when they are creating with technology on their own or as part of a collaborative project. Instead of rolling out separate technology lessons to teach skills like font formatting, we are giving children authentic experiences to learn them.

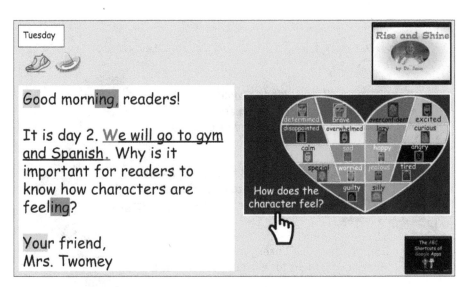

Children can show their thinking by using text formatting
options to recognize reading strategies (i.e., word chunking)
or print concepts (identifying a complete sentence).

Children have the chance to learn and practice using tools in a safe space where they have a personal investment in communicating their thinking. They quickly learn shortcuts for bolding, italicizing, or underlining text. They learn to change text color and highlight using customized colors. They learn how to use Ctrl+F to search for and recognize how many letters, words, and punctuation marks there are in a given Morning Message. They learn how to find and insert images to expand ideas. Be ready for kids to help you learn new tips and tricks for working in Google Slides, as they have limitless curiosity about how to express their thinking in a visual format. You can teach your students about other ways to tweak their writing by using *The ABC Shortcuts of Google Apps* e-book.

Innovating Play Bonus Resources:
Find more at innovatingplay.world/abcshortcuts

10 Morning Message Tips from Jessica

1 Play with different kinds of pointers! The projected screen can create the opportunity for magical shadow pointers.

2 Create a variety of master slides to meet the needs of different Morning Messages.

3 Change the colored background of the Morning Messages for each day of the week.

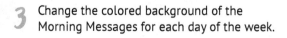

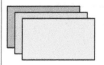

4 Group Morning Messages in a slide deck with other pieces that will be used for facilitation.

5 Add multiple slides as needed. This prevents crowding visuals.

6 Find a workflow that feels good, so ideas and skills are clear and connected. I wrote Morning Messages after I planned for the week.

7 Allow yourself to create a message for any content area or time of the day.

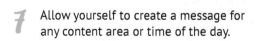

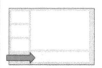

8 Use the Notes section to leave notes for collaborating teachers.

9 Find special-occasion add-ons (GIFs, rainbow font, etc.).

10 Be willing to change up and learn new ways to enhance your Morning Message!

Of all of the aspects of Morning Message that have the potential for transformation, the ability to move the Morning Message beyond the walls of the classroom may be the most pivotal. The message written on chart paper speaks to the community of learners in a single physical space; the Morning Message in Google Slides can speak to a community of learners as it exists anywhere.

One of the clearest examples of this is the way Jessica shared her Morning Message slides with a special education teacher to balance both pull-out and push-in experiences to meet the needs of specific learners.[2] Jessica used Google Slides' "share" feature to grant the teacher access to view the Morning Message slides so that they could both use them with their shared students. This enabled students who were being pulled out during the Morning Message time the ability to see, in real time, how the message was being manipulated in the classroom, while experiencing the specific kinds of learning they needed in an alternative space.

In addition to extending the message this way, the slides were also shared between buddy classrooms, with families for follow-up, and with students who were absent from school. (Sharing was made possible via Seesaw, although other platforms could be used.) Now, not only could children revisit the Morning Message in the classroom, they could revisit it beyond the physical space and transfer their learning to other people and places in their world.

One of the key elements of a yearlong collaboration with young children is taking advantage of small moments and common routines to continuously plant seeds for shared learning. Just as Christine used the idea of the Wish You Well Heart to create a shared experience between classrooms, Jessica presented the Morning Message as a way to create another shared experience. As the Morning Message would set the tone for that day's lessons and explorations in the classroom, it made sense that creating a message that could be used in both classrooms would help to clarify connections the students would make. For example,

---

2   Pull-out and push-in experiences are typically carried out by support or special education teachers to accommodate the needs of specific learners in and out of the classroom.

many of our collaborative projects (presented later in the book) were built on connections that were made in smaller ways throughout the week. The Morning Message ensured that our classes would have a common language and understanding as we moved toward a specific collaboration. Creating the Morning Message within a digital format meant that we could plan and contribute ideas together and then move the final pieces into each of the message slides specifically customized to work within our space.

Shifting from a paper space to a digital space does not take away the human experience surrounding the Morning Message. In fact, it can open up rich learning options that can be experienced in individual classrooms while creating common ground for all children involved in a collaboration. The addition of photos, music, video, images, and varied text produces a visceral reaction that deeply impacts children's sense of community and their connection to learning. In our experience, children became extremely protective of the Morning Message time as a whole. They treated each experience with respect, as it offered safety and comfort through the predictable format while always piquing their curiosity about how they would experience learning next.

Facilitation Questions for Morning Message

TRADITIONAL WITH A POSTER

- How does the pointer help us to show what good readers do when they read?
- What did you notice about the morning message today? Who would like to be a teacher and use the marker to show us what is happening in your brain as a reader?
- Who would like the chance to be a reader by setting a reading goal and reading the message on their own?
- Who would like the chance to be a leader by tracking the message for us again while we read the words together?
- What compliments or feedback can you give to our reader or leader to recognize his or her effort as a reader?

ENHANCED BY GOOGLE SLIDES

- How can we show our thinking as readers by using the tools in Google Slides?
- Which tools would you like to use to show your thinking? Why is that an effective tool for showing our thinking? Have you seen authors use that tool in books?
- Are there any keyboard shortcuts we can use to help us show our thinking?
- What is the connection between the video/image in the message and the words?
- Why is it important to explore ideas in different ways? What are some ways that people communicate ideas beyond printed words?

TRANSFORMED BY COLLABORATING WITH ANOTHER CLASS

- What are the ideas in our message that are specific to our classroom? How do you know that these ideas might only apply to us?
- What are the big ideas in our message that we can connect to our work with our buddies?
- If our buddies are reading the same message today, what does it tell us about their learning?
- Would we need to approach our learning differently because of the differences in our spaces? Why or why not?
- What kinds of projects might we be able to do together this week? What steps would we need to take to make that collaborative experience work between classrooms that are far away from each other?

Innovating Play Bonus Resources: Find more at innovatingplay.world/mmfocusoptions

Bringing the Ritual into Student Play

The most amazing classroom routines are those that are so carefully woven together that ownership continuously and seamlessly transfers to the students. For older students, this shift may happen quickly. For younger children, it is often a gradual release. Either way, the true measure of a strong and meaningful ritual or routine is the degree to which it belongs to the students.

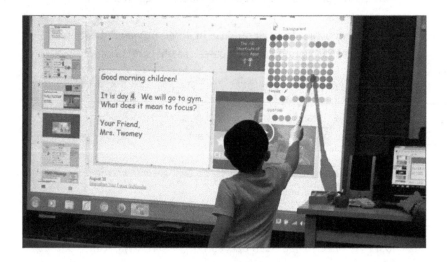

As we shifted our Morning Message to Google Slides, we gave careful attention to the ways in which children participated in the experience. Morning Message jobs (like being teachers to share what they know) are among the most popular experiences in the classroom. The children "hire" each other as helpers by recognizing who has earned the responsibility and considering fairness in the classroom.

As children pass the reading fairies to each other to perform different tasks within the message, you will clearly hear the language of the classroom that the children have nurtured together:

- "I am a girl, so I will be fair and offer the job to a boy."
- "I noticed that ___ has been focused and calm. Would you like the job?"

- "I'm looking for someone that is sitting safely, looking at me, and being respectful."
- "I appreciate the way ___ was quiet when it was my turn. I would like to offer you the job."
- "I heard that ___ was feeling sad during the Feelings Check-In. I'd like to share this job with you."

Connecting Literacy to the Ritual

In addition to allowing children to demonstrate their thinking via the tools in Google Slides, the message became a space in which children could both support each other and set and work toward learning goals. Each day, a child selected by one of his or her peers was given the choice of either being a "reader" (reading the message to the class independently) or a "leader" (using the reading fairies to point to the words as the class reads together). That child then selected a personal goal to work on through the message. Goals included working on fluency, expression, volume, pacing, sight words, making sure what we say matches what we see, or specific reading strategy use. Children really tuned in to each other as they listened, giving a thumbs up (meaning "You got it!") or a thumb to the side (meaning "You are working toward your goal—we believe in you!"). The whole experience not only gave students time to shine during their special moments with the message, but also helped them to recognize the growth of their peers. They offered specific and meaningful feedback to each other, providing evidence of successes and acknowledgment of their willingness to take risks as growing learners.

Another benefit of shifting away from chart paper and moving to slides projected onto a bigger space is that it presents opportunities for children to see larger print. In Google Slides, text options allow us to easily manipulate font, size of text, and text features (bold, italics, underline, color). Similar to the big book experience in which children are exposed to print on a larger scale to simulate the lap-reading experience, the Morning Message on Google Slides increases exposure to book-like text. This creates an ideal opportunity for modeling print concepts for emergent readers.

In addition to manipulating text for the Morning Message, we use the echo reading strategy to support readers, as well. The teacher reads one sentence at a time while pointing to each word with the reading fairies. Children then have the opportunity to read the sentence back while the teacher tracks the print once again. This creates a safe reading experience, allowing all children to see and hear themselves as successful readers from the very beginning. The playing field is leveled as children have equal exposure and interaction with the text.

One thing we quickly learned when shifting to the Google Slides format was that we would need to play with the placement of text based on where it falls in the projected area. This took some trial and error, so we recommend testing it out and seeing where the print lands in your space before rolling out these slides with the kids. Is the font large enough? Are the words in the message within reach for the kids to point to when interacting with it? As you begin to explore the Morning Message with your students, empower them to be part of the process. Encouraging students to find learning spaces that work for them as you participate in the Morning Message together creates a collective mindset of problem-solving and engagement.

The Last Day of Morning Message: Jessica's Reflection

During the first year of presenting the Morning Message in Google Slides, the message went through many transformations. From text placement to customized layouts, the process was richly rewarding from both teacher and student perspectives. As the year went on, the feeling and flow of the Morning Message became clearer. The deep connection the children were developing as part of the process was evident to anyone who walked in the room. People who visited our classroom would walk away glowing with the lovely feeling of what they had just seen and experienced through the Morning Message. It often took on the feeling of a movie scene, with moments of such perfection that they simply took our breath away.

Eventually, we came to realize that Morning Message had gone from a routine to an adventure thanks to the fuller sensations that come with multimedia experiences. There were times when we would get lost in songs, the beauty of an image, or the feeling of movement that came through video. We marveled at the way children took on the responsibilities of the message and saw their own growth and the growth of their friends. All of these realizations turned into the knowledge that if we quietly backed out of the classroom, these five- and six-year-old children would know how to carry on, where to click, and how to discover without us.

We entered the last Morning Message of the school year with joy and sadness, as this was a routine that we had all come to love together. We woke the fairies for the last time as the children sang to them. Deep belly laughs came when they saw the otter GIF that I had added to the message to cheer them on and congratulate them.

I had inserted a slide with twenty different videos that had been included in the Morning Message throughout the year. Throughout the day, I invited children to choose a favorite video, identify what song it was, and share the connected experience and a special memory from something we did during that learning time. Without fail, every child I pulled aside correctly identified the song, knew exactly which thematic or literature connection it represented, and recalled experience after experience that we had participated in together. They remembered what they had written about, what they had created, what they had read, games they had played, and new vocabulary, concepts, skills, and strategies they had learned. My heart beamed with joy as I saw that the Morning Message had become a daily routine and learning space from which all other classroom experiences blossomed, collectively forming the learning journey.

Extended Learning Experience with Families

The Morning Messages contains important information and sets up a shared experience to communicate about the day ahead. After the message is manipulated by the teacher and students, it holds a record of the thinking and discoveries children made as readers during that time. When the message existed on paper only in the classroom, children naturally sought out opportunities to revisit the chart independently throughout the day. After shifting the message to a digital format, it took on a new life. It can easily be shared with families, which presents ways to revisit and support conversations at home. Together, children can work with family members to continue to develop skills and strategies and process information. While caregivers once had to rely on asking what the child did at school that day, they now have the message to complement whatever their child tells them. Children can work with family members to articulate ideas about the highlighted elements or changes to text within the message and what they represent. Together, family members can view images, sing songs, or listen to video read-alouds that may have been inserted in the message. Moreover, children can transfer specific language and vocabulary outside the classroom, as access to the message brings daily school and home experiences together.

We found that one of the easiest ways to share the Morning Message was to simply create a separate slide deck into which any messages could be copied and to publish that deck online. We then added to the slide deck throughout the year. Having a separate space that is shared with families also gave us, as teachers, freedom in deciding which messages to share. To ensure families know when a new Morning Message has been added to the slide deck, an announcement or post via a communication tool is used.[3] We have had several parents thank us for giving them access to these resources, which make them feel included in their child's day. They have enjoyed singing, learning, and playing with their children in new ways due to being able to access our Morning Messages.

Learning with the #InnovatingPlay Community

What tips do you have for facilitating or creating Morning Messages? What components of your Morning Message do you and the kids enjoy?

innovatingplay.world/bookq3

---

3   Digital communication tools are platforms that allow teachers to post information, share student learning, and directly message families.

Innovating Play in the Curriculum

orning routines and rituals often focus on establishing safety and security within the learning community. As the day progresses, we develop routines for content areas that are driven by academic expectations and standards. This does not mean that the concepts in the routines need to become dry and detached from connection and meaning.

> Reflecting on and reconsidering everyday routines in all areas gives us the opportunity to discover new ways to approach learning with connection.

We recognize that teachers all have different areas of growth and comfort levels, especially in the area of innovating with technology. In an effort to offer different levels of support, this section is dedicated to letting you into the thinking behind our work. It is our hope that by sharing our thinking, we will help each teacher to develop a mindset that inspires even more creative energy in the classroom.

Rather than starting with technology, all of the experiences we are about to share have unfolded from the big-picture ideas that we value as educators. Here are some of the types of questions that we kept in mind as we set out to develop a foundation for broadening literacy, math, and science routines:

- How can we support children in making deeper connections to the experience of reading?
- How do we bridge the worlds of books and digital media?
- How do we safely and thoughtfully simulate the experiences of consuming visual information and text that are out in the world?
- How can we support the development of a mathematical and scientific mindset that expands the natural connections children make to learning in the world?
- How can we use technology to reframe and more actively include learners in the collection and analysis of data?
- Why is it important to collect multiple sets of data? How can we easily include meaningful data from multiple sources in order to compare and contrast, ask questions, and draw conclusions?
- As districts across the country work to implement Next Generation Science Standards (NGSS), how can we use free tools to approach instruction with depth and authenticity?
- How can we use the structure of daily routines to create rich context for literacy, along with mathematical and scientific application of ideas?
- How does perspective shift when we move beyond observing what is in front of us to a larger view of the world?

As the questions driving our decisions became clearer, we created a foundation we could draw upon as we developed the practical facilitation of the experience. We zeroed in on our big ideas for routines across curricular areas, which are as follows:

- Literacy experiences are often built upon a series of connections that can be experienced, captured, documented, and extended through digital tools.
- Digital literacy represents an important element of learning that should be included in the process of developing emergent literacy skills and strategies.
- Digital tools offer multiple ways for children to collect and visualize information.

- Virtual spaces open up opportunities for collaboration between classrooms in order to communicate and analyze multiple sets of data. Using multimedia tools to collect information allows children to create a window into their immediate world that can be shared with others.
- Collaborative collection and sharing of data allow children to interpret on a local and global scale, supporting them in becoming thinkers beyond the walls of the classroom.

Taking time to ask questions and identify the big ideas that can focus your innovation efforts is an empowering approach for educators. It will not only help you to create a meaningful course of action but will constantly keep you and your students focused as you carry out these routines on a daily basis. This mindset is particularly important for routines that will be revisited every day of the school year. It is through the big ideas that we ensure our instruction continues to develop and grow in ways that meet our students' needs on all levels, support the transfer of learning to the larger world, and create exciting and joyful moments in and beyond our classrooms each and every day.

Applying the Mindset and Lesson Planning

In this section of the book you will see different ways that we use the Innovating Play Cycle to facilitate learning experiences across the curriculum. We will share how we reimagine traditional literacy approaches as we **connect** with texts, ideas, and each other. We apply the idea of **wonder** to delve deeper into emergent literacy skills, strategies, and concepts. We take our curiosity beyond the idea of comprehension and pave the way for children to **play** with books and stories. Through this approach, they develop deeper personal connections to the texts and contribute to collaborative digital creations within and between classrooms. Digital class books, videos, and projects reflect the rich experiences in which the children **discover** as active participants and creators.

As we develop daily routines and special projects in areas of literacy, math, and science, we constantly return to the Innovating Play Cycle to ground these learning experiences. While we talk you through the application of the process for daily routines such as the days of school or weather collaboration, we also offer examples of specific projects for which a lesson plan framework is provided in the resources section. This lesson plan is meant to guide the planning of focused curricular projects between classes in order to ensure a rich, stand-alone experience. While shared routines are modeled with the Innovating Play Cycle in mind, specific experiences (particularly in the areas of math and science) can be developed by using the focus questions within the lesson plan as guidance.

Literacy

I n every classroom, across grade levels and content areas, literacy plays an important role in absorbing and communicating information and experiences. We often consider literacy as it relates to the understanding, processing, and sharing of ideas through print. However, as the digital landscape continues to develop, new possibilities for redefining literacy are beginning to unfold. With this shift comes the opportunity to consider what this perspective means in schools as we support young children as growing readers and writers. We now ask ourselves how we can bridge children's exposure to print and digital media so that they develop a rich literacy perspective in their world.

When we transfer the experience of literacy beyond the words in a book, we show children that stories and ideas matter because they are reflections of our world and our imaginations. If we just teach skills and strategies using print books, that's all children may see. However, we want them to experience why books—or ideas expressed through any medium—are important. If we limit reading to text on paper, we limit students' understanding of the world in which they live. Print is just one way ideas are communicated. In order to successfully engage and participate within the world, children need to learn to receive and express ideas in multiple ways. That is what we give children in Extended Reading.

Literacy Instruction through Extended Reading

While we focus largely on tech integration throughout this book, we also want to give the experiences we offer context and meaning in order to paint the bigger picture of learning. When we began to develop the framework that would guide our daily collaboration and allow us to explore new possibilities together, we needed to look closely at the traditional experiences that occurred in each portion of our day. As we compared our classroom approaches, we explored options for redefining our literacy block to create experiences that could be facilitated within and between our classrooms. Here we recognized the need to build upon the traditional approach of shared reading.[1] We first noted the important elements of a shared reading experience that we would maintain in our practices. Among these was the need to preserve a lap-reading experience for young children; to do this, we would continue to simulate it by using books in which print and pictures could be clearly viewed by all children (whether this was a hands-on big book or a digital version on a screen). We also wanted to maintain the repeated exposure to the same text throughout the week to allow the children to develop skills and strategies by closely analyzing the text. While we valued the developmentally appropriate practices of the shared reading approach, we wanted to further explore the role that digital media and technology play in emergent literacy. In taking this approach, we would support practices that allowed for the application of skills and strategies, along with analysis of digitally communicated ideas, including multimedia formats. Equally important would be exploring the opportunity to use digital tools to extend understanding of stories through personalized and collaborative creation. This meant that reading would not only

---

1 Shared reading is an instructional approach that mimics home reading experiences in a group setting for young children. (Definition taken from Barbara Honchell & Melissa Schulz, "Engaging Young Readers with Text through Shared Reading Experiences," *Journal of Inquiry & Action in Education* 4 no. 3 (2012): 59–67.)

be shared but extended to encompass a broader definition of literacy. We decided to refer to this part of our day as Extended Reading.

In our Extended Reading lessons, each tech extension represents a piece of the instructional flow that happens throughout any given week in the classroom. When we plan our literacy block, a focus text or featured concept is selected to be revisited throughout the week. This allows for rich instructional opportunities that create a safe space for both guidance and discovery. Materials may include anything from a district-mandated book to a familiar song, nursery rhyme, or teacher-selected text. It could be fiction or nonfiction and can certainly cross content areas. The idea is to choose a text or concept that works for your population of students and allows for rich opportunities that can extend reading beyond the book in a variety of ways.

Since the flow of our literacy experiences is maintained on both a daily and weekly basis, the lesson-planning template we use for collaboration on these experiences looks different from the Innovating Play lesson plan that we will share for more specific projects in Chapters 5 and 6. However, the Innovating Play Cycle is embedded in the development of all Extended Reading experiences. Before we look closely at our weekly literacy schedule and offer examples of Extended Reading in action, we will share how the Innovating Play Cycle is embedded in the development of lessons and experiences throughout the week.

Connect

Each Extended Reading experience is based on a focus text or concept that serves as a point of connection. The connection is established as the week begins and is often introduced through the Morning Message, as outlined in Chapter 3. Since the messages are developed between collaborating classes, we found this to be a very effective way to start to establish common learning points before any specific collaborative literacy projects are introduced. Our students have come to understand that it is quite likely that when one class is working with a specific text or concept, the other class could very well be working on the same thing! Because we have established this connected culture, children will often ask, "Is our buddy class reading this story too?" This understanding also prompts rich conversations on the perspective of readers and the identification of an audience for writers. For example, if we are reading a book about winter we might draw the children's attention to how the experience of a reader in California will be different from the experience of a reader in New Jersey. This helps young children see the power of books to communicate and the importance of making connections to personal experience as we read books and gather information.

Wonder

The element of wonder is present as we embark on a new reading adventure together and delve deeper into vocabulary development within a text. Together we wonder what words mean and why the word choice was important to the author. We wonder about how words apply to our world and how we can use strategies to make sense of unknown words in text. We wonder what happens in our brains as readers, and we break down these ideas throughout the lessons in any given week. Wonder is the element that engages readers and supports critical thinking as we explore communication and ideas in text and other multimedia formats together. It is also what leads us to the next phase of Extended Reading as we wonder: How can we play with this story?

Play

The play portion of Extended Reading departs slightly from traditional reading instruction and is often what makes the experience special. Here our curiosity has inspired us to move beyond the words on the page or the images on a screen, which are communicated by the author and illustrator alone. This is where we take the opportunity to deepen personal connection with the text by building experiences that allow children to visualize, create, and engage as active participants in a literacy experience. This is where technology offers us tools that can immerse children in texts in ways that were not possible in the past. Through Extended Reading, children become creators of and contributors to a shared literacy experience within and between collaborating classrooms.

Discover

Every Extended Reading experience or creation is meant to broaden each child's concept of literacy as it applies to themselves, the world, and a variety of texts. In Chapter 9 we will address this idea further as we show the ways in which many of our Extended Reading creations can be used to share discoveries with families and elsewhere beyond the classroom. In order to facilitate these experiences, we generally follow the same flow for instruction each week. Although the objectives and standards that are covered change, the focus areas tend to stay consistent.

While the flow and consistency help us to ensure that instruction remains balanced, we also consider the need to break the lessons up differently when necessary. For example, some retelling experiences need to be built from pieces that will be experienced and completed throughout the course of the week or even several weeks. You will also see how we explore the idea of collaborative literacy through extended reading in one of the sample experiences provided in this chapter. No matter what the flow of instruction is, we approach each week with excitement to both maintain organization and embrace texts and literacy concepts in a variety of innovative ways.

In this section we share several examples of what Extended Reading experiences have looked like in our classrooms. Although we share experiences, templates, and resources, we encourage you to use these examples as inspiration for developing your own experiences. As you explore, here are some questions to keep in mind:

- How does this experience support children in making deeper connections to the processes of reading, writing, and communicating?
- How does this experience bridge the worlds of books and digital media?
- How does this experience safely and thoughtfully simulate the intake of visual information and text that occurs out in the world?

Balanced Literacy Through Extended Reading

MONDAY

EXPERIENCE THE STORY

Take time to enjoy the story together! Allow children time to hear, ponder, discuss, and make personal and text-to-text connections.

TUESDAY

VOCABULARY BUILDING

Focus on building language and exposure to rich vocabulary found within the text.

WEDNESDAY

PHRASING AND FLUENCY

Repeated exposure to the same text throughout the week allows all readers to hear and practice appropriate expression and flow of communication.

THURSDAY

PHONEMIC AWARENESS/PHONICS

Playing with oral language is key for emergent readers. More advanced readers benefit from the opportunity to focus on word patterns to support further literacy development.

FRIDAY

RETELLING

Rounding out the week by allowing children to retell the story in creative ways ensures that they have the opportunity to solidify comprehension and understanding of events and/or information.

For young children, Extended Reading builds on the concept of shared reading. This process is meant to simulate the lap-reading experience between child and caregiver. It is a safe approach to literacy that allows children to connect the skills and strategies that we are building within a real and meaningful text. As we redefine this experience, we consider ways to bridge the worlds of print and digital media so that children develop a rich perspective on literacy in their world. While we focus on work with emergent readers, the concept of Extended Reading can easily transfer to literacy instruction for all readers across grades and content areas. As you consider points of connection for your students, here are some of the areas we encourage you to recognize:

- Connection between the teacher and student in making reading a personal and safe experience
- Student-to-student connection as they engage in text together in the classroom
- Student-to-student connection as they engage in experiences between classrooms
- Connection between skills and strategies within the text rather than in isolation
- Personal connections that the student makes between the text and prior knowledge and experience
- Connection of the content to the bigger project, area of focus, or theme that is being explored

One of the greatest gifts we can give young readers and writers is a deep connection to why their ideas and thoughts matter in the world. When we take time to personalize literacy experiences, we allow children to own the experiences and motivate them to want to develop their ideas through reading and writing. By extending reading beyond the book, we help children to see and feel the joy, the connection, and the possibilities that they possess as authentic learners, thinkers, and creators.

In order to facilitate rich experiences, there are many elements to consider. Designing experiences with technology means considering everything within the context of the people, space, goals, and resources available. Check out the "Tips for Developing Extended Reading Experiences through Technology" infographic for ideas on how to support you in your design process.

Tips for Developing Extended Reading Experiences Through Technology

 Be ready to see learning opportunities everywhere! Pay attention to holidays, events, engaging texts, and favorite songs, and embrace them as teachable opportunities for Extended Reading.

Work with your district curriculum. Extended Reading is another way to instruct, imagine, offer opportunities, and reach students. Start with what you have, then imagine possibilities.

 Tune in to your students' strengths, talents, interests, and challenges. Consider Extended Reading experiences as ways to develop and meet students' needs.

Invite your tech coach to see the context of learning within your grade level and utilize his or her expertise to imagine new possibilities. Maintain best practices and elevate them!

 Develop comfort with open-ended tech tools. Having a strong foundation and understanding of a handful of open-ended tools will help to provide lots of options for extensions.

Choose tools that work together. Often Extended Reading experiences need to be built, created, and communicated by weaving tools together. Don't be afraid to app smash!

 Always consider the context of your experiences. Use Connected Play, Morning Message, and Extended Reading times to complement each other and weave your days/weeks together.

Collaborate with other educators. Create a safe space to put all ideas out on the table. The process and end product will be better when you acknowledge and tap into the talents of others.

 **Buddy up with a class!** Whether it's in your building or across the country, consider how student collaboration brings authentic audience and connection opportunities.

Let families in! Share Extended Reading experiences to model developmentally appropriate use of technology and literacy.

The Language of Stories: Playing with Characters and Setting to Create a Class Book

As often as we can, we connect student interests, holidays, or even school spirit weeks to learning opportunities. During the month of October, as five-year-old excitement was building for our upcoming Halloween celebrations, we wondered how we could connect our classes in their energy for the holiday event. Instead of just "making it through" the holiday and returning to learning afterward, we thought about how we could embrace the opportunity to connect and teach with the experience rather than working around it. We saw the ways in which children dressing up would mean that their imaginations were prepped for possibilities. We saw opportunities that could emerge from Halloween day, when many children in the class would attempt to become a character in their hearts and minds as they stepped into their costumes and came to school. Furthermore, children would naturally want to tell stories, imagine details, and make connections. This was an authentic literacy experience waiting to happen if we could capture what was right in front of us! With these ideas in mind, we set out to build context, nurture connections, and not only bring reading into the experience but go beyond the book as well.

We carefully looked for a text that was accessible to both classes and appropriate for kindergartners early in the year. Using the leveled book *Halloween Costumes* from Reading A-Z, we were able to initiate a conventional shared reading experience focused on story pattern, high-frequency words, and the role of character and setting within the story.[2] Our goal was to then take the experience further and engage children in these concepts by extending reading beyond the book.

To continue to break down this experience, let's consider what the next phases of this project look like through the Innovating Play Cycle

---

2   Leveling systems are used to organize a collection of books to ensure that readers are working at appropriate instructional levels and to guide instruction.

from both the student and teacher perspectives. When working with a collaborating class, there are multiple points of connection to consider. We began by connecting the instructional focuses and academic objectives that needed to be covered to ensure we would be meeting curricular expectations for the entire population of students. Once that was in place, we spent time in the wonder part of the Innovating Play Cycle to consider the points of connection that would need to happen between teachers to bring the experience to life. We asked these questions:

- What do we need to do in each of our classrooms to contribute to the project as a whole?
- Which parts of the project are best completed individually, on our own time?
- Which parts are best completed together during real-time collaboration?
- What is our timeline for completion?
- What are the digital and physical materials we will each need to access?

As Halloween day brings high energy levels and considerable excitement, we knew we would each need to make sure that the setup for this experience was prepared ahead of time. It was essential that we complete the necessary steps with the children during the course of the day while they were wearing their costumes. As each child would play the role of a character in our collaborative class book, we needed to capture a picture of each one against a green screen in the classroom. After using a background removal tool, such as remove.bg, we then saved the children's images so that they could be added to our project later. Working independently for this part of the project, we each organized our pictures in a table in Google Docs so that we would be able to work efficiently through the next steps of creation together. When working with a collaborating class in a different space (and especially in a different time zone), setting up an efficient workflow for each teacher's contributions is critical.

The next phase of the project happened after the school day was finished for both classes. It was time for us to move to the next phase

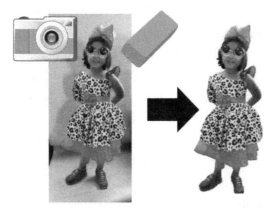

of the Innovating Play Cycle and turn to play as teachers! With each of our Google Docs tables of photos open in one tab, we created a shared Google Slides deck in another. Together, we talked about common characters we had and searched for background images we could use that would match each type of character. Witches were added to the spooky forest slide, superheroes were given a sky to fly through, and mermaids and sharks found a home in the ocean. What would have been separate holiday celebrations in each school became an opportunity to create a shared play space for children on opposite sides of the country to see their imaginations come to life together.

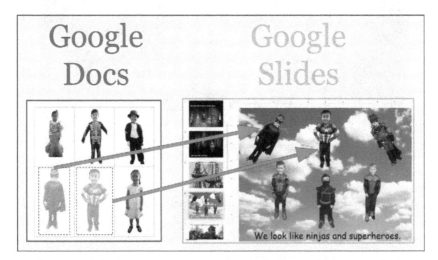

It was helpful to each have our own Google Doc with our own kids so we could do a headcount. We cut the images of the students and pasted them into our shared Google Slides space. An empty Google Doc meant everyone had been included in the Google Slides space.

We were very excited to surprise each of our classes with this special new class book that was based on the shared text we had explored. While the slides would be printed to create a physical book we would keep in our classrooms, we also knew that our young readers would benefit from hearing this repetitive text read to them; by doing this, we would be helping them connect oral language to print with this personalized text. We also recognized the opportunity to highlight the value of a multimedia approach to literacy. As a result, we brought the class book to another level of play by creating a listening center for the children to enjoy in the classroom. For the listening center, we downloaded each slide as a PNG and inserted it into an Adobe Spark video. We then took turns reading each page so that the children would be able to hear both their California and their New Jersey teachers' voices reading to them. Another benefit was that this version of our project could easily be shared with families, deepening the connection between our classes by bringing the children's shared experiences into their homes.

As both the physical and the listening-center versions of our books were shared with the children, their reactions sparked further levels of play. This book quickly became a favorite in both classrooms as the children connected with peers who shared their setting. Conversations began about the details of what might actually happen on each page. Children returned to the book during free time to solidify their play story ideas and to look for evidence of what they could continue to develop with their imaginations. They snuggled up in the reading corner to listen to their story told again, and families shared their delight at this magical project.

In the weeks following the creation and sharing of our class book, we continued to integrate literacy experiences that stemmed from this project. The tables that we had originally used to organize student photos were edited to create a resource board for character types. Simply labeling the type of character in each photo created a personalized resource that children could turn to when writing their own stories. Similarly, a resource board of settings was created by inserting the background images into a table and labeling each setting. These resources were printed, laminated, and added to our writing center to support children as they wrote independently. We noted that children were more likely to include a variety of characters and detailed settings due to the personalized nature of these resource boards and the experience connected with their creation.

Settings		Characters	
stage	spooky forest	famous characters	witches
pirate ship	old house	pirates	skeletons and vampires
circus	ocean	ringmaster	community helpers
castle	magical world	ninjas and superheros	magical creatures
sky	town	princesses and dragons	sea creatures

In building this experience together we had the opportunity to discover what would happen when we took a shared experience, such as a Halloween celebration in the classroom, and used it as a starting point to extend children's ideas about imagination, character, setting, and storytelling. We learned the potential of playing together, as teachers and students, to create a rich learning experience that extends reading in ways that make literacy seem real, personal, and magical.

From a technology integration perspective, we used a variety of tools including photo editing apps, Google Docs, Google Slides, and Adobe Spark. The following benefits were clearly observed and demonstrated during this experience:

- High levels of authentic engagement due to the use of images of the children within the experience
- Deeper levels of thinking on story elements such as character and setting, and the role of each in telling a story through creation and manipulation of images
- Collaborative creation and respect for digital spaces
- Connection of ideas between the text and experiences of collaborative and independent writing
- Natural motivation for story development and expression of ideas
- Connection to teachers beyond the classroom through a collaborative read-aloud of the book
- Development of empathy and connection beyond the immediate environment
- Motivation through personalization of the storytelling experience

In Extended Reading there is a flow between the digital world and the physical world of print. The best experiences will weave the two together and help children to be the creators of literacy experiences rather than simply passive consumers. By the end of this project, children had a tangible classroom book and writing resources in their hands that allowed them to experience reading and writing as extensions of themselves. The most meaningful projects will allow students to engage with books, communication, imagination, and storytelling. The learning that sticks with them will most likely come from opportunities that we take to reflect back to them the ways in which they are capable, important contributors to the learning process.

Innovating Play Bonus Resources:
Find more at innovatingplay.world/halloween

Playing with Words Centers

Many teachers offer word work center experiences in their classrooms to support literacy instruction in small groups or for independent readers.[3] We love using these kinds of experiences as a way to broaden exposure and experiences for learners. Using the Extended Reading text as a guide, we develop playing with words centers through which the children rotate over the course of the week. During this time, we are able to meet with small groups for guided reading or individual reading conferences. A variety of types of experiences that support learning styles and engagement provide additional opportunities to deepen children's sense of connection with their learning. For example, personal data folders can allow children to access "just right" sight words to ensure appropriate differentiation through open-ended thematic activities.[4] When children create their words with a sensory material (like sand) or complete a hands-on activity, technology can be used for documentation and accountability. This presents the opportunity to give meaningful feedback to children and families. On that note, play boards (as shown below) are created in Google Slides to organize and facilitate hands-on, small-group experiences.

---

3   Word work is a hands-on time to explore alphabet knowledge, phonemic awareness, word patterns, spellings, and vocabulary development.

4   Students use personal data folders to keep track of their own learning, set personal goals, and reflect on and keep track of their progress. In an early education classroom, this can include letters, sounds, and sight words. "Just right" words refer to the sight words a child might be focusing on at any given time and can vary from student to student.

Playing with Words

HOW DO LETTERS MAKE WORDS?
HOW DO READERS LEARN NEW WORDS?

Children play a Hide-and-Seek Monster Sight Word Game. Blank boards allow children to personalize the experience with "just right" words.

Children use paint bags and cotton swabs to practice sight words using a multisensory approach.

Salt trays with Halloween confetti allow children to practice forming letters and words. Using photo and audio tools in Seesaw, students photograph and record spelling and reading the word.

Children use spider rings and monster finger pointers (available on Amazon) to practice reading words in Guided Reading texts.

Children use thematic books to explore letters and words. A recording sheet is used to color when a word or letter is identified in a text.

Innovating Play Bonus Resources: Find more at innovatingplay.world/playingwithwordscenters

Visualization and Imagination: An Invitation to Play in the Snow

One of the greatest gifts we can give children as we introduce them to technology is the ability to work side by side and imagine the impossible together. As Christine prepared for her first visit to the classroom in New Jersey, we knew we had a new kind of opportunity to embrace this idea.

The idea for this project stemmed from a writing prompt that children in Christine's class would be completing in January asking them to write about winter. Depending on the background knowledge of the child, the season of winter could mean many things. Winter in Christine's region of California looks quite different from winter in New Jersey. As we brought our classes together throughout the year, we often noticed the ways in which children's understanding of the larger world was deepened through our shared experiences. In the past this had come in the form of videos, books, live chats, collaborative apps, and shared hands-on experiences. This time we wanted to support the children in taking what they had learned about winter weather and truly personalizing the experience. It was from this objective that the Invitation to Play in the Snow was born.

As part of our author study of Jan Brett, we focused on the book *The Mitten*. This led to discussions of winter clothing and what it is like to play in the snow. As the children in New Jersey had many experiences with playing in the snow, they were able to tap into prior knowledge. The experience for the children in California was quite different, as they had to "imagine" what it would be like to play in snow. While Christine was visiting the children in New Jersey, she was excited to begin facilitating a shared project that would allow her to bring the experience of snow back to her classroom.

The project began by having the New Jersey children dress up in their winter gear and taking "action shot" pictures of each child in front of a blank wall. Each child chose their pose based on how they would want to play with their California buddy in the snow—for instance by having a snowball fight, ice skating, building a snowman, or making snow angels. By removing the background (using remove.bg), we created an image that was easily inserted into winter-themed Google Slides.

As we added the children's pictures onto the Google Slides background, we projected them so that the children could see the process. During the time the photos were taken the children were participating in open-ended play around the classroom. One of the play areas included wooden blocks, a dollhouse, and winter props. As the winter action photos were displayed, we noticed the ways in which the children's play in the block center was particularly impacted. They began delving deeper into their language and extending their learning by telling stories of the characters in the snow. They used props to add icicles and snow to their block house as they invited all of the friends (California and New Jersey block people) into their stories. Their ability to visualize and communicate story ideas was evident through their block play. Later, we would see the ways in which this opportunity to experience

visual and hands-on learning would impact their experience as writers.

When Christine returned to her classroom, she revealed the waiting Kmail (explained in greater detail later in the chapter) from the New Jersey class inviting the children in California to play in the snow too. She repeated the process, allowing the children to dress up in winter gear and pose for their snow scene. The children looked carefully at their buddy waiting for them in the snow and had to determine the action that would match what was happening in the snow setting. This allowed the children in California to make deeper connections to what it might look like to actually be in the snow by connecting movement and visual experiences.

While the New Jersey children were waiting for their buddies to join them in the snow, Jessica used a copy of the snow slides for a center experience. Children used a snow clothes resource and Word Art to add labels below the pictures of themselves in the snow.

Once all of the children finally joined each other in snow scenes, the snow pictures were downloaded and printed out for each of the children. Using paper and pencil, they were able to explore ideas as they wrote about playing with their buddies in the snow.

As we consider possibilities for play, technology gives us tools to visualize things that may seem impossible. Hopping on a plane and meeting for a field trip to play in the snow was not possible for our classes (although it was certainly a suggestion from the children as we wondered about ways to play together). Still, we found a way to deeply imagine and to immerse students in that experience through the intentional use of technology.

Through the creation of and participation in these experiences, children are able to deepen their ability to visualize and explore ideas. As children had the opportunity to see themselves in the snow with their buddies 2,500 miles away, they also saw the limitless possibilities and potential for what they could create and experience together. This ability to visualize and imagine is central to the quality of play and learning experiences.

It is through rich play that young children begin to prepare for later learning by creating mental images. The ability to visualize and hold mental images is necessary for reading, writing, mathematics, science, design thinking, and problem-solving. Instead of allowing technology to limit the children's imaginations, we can use the tools at our fingertips to help their imaginations flourish. When we take time to value and capture imagination through technology, we let kids know that their experiences matter. Their contributions matter. Their learning matters in the classroom and beyond.

Innovating Play Bonus Resources:
Find more at innovatingplay.world/snow

Spotlight on Kmail

How do children see and experience our world? As educators we must continuously reassess the world in which we live and take note of the ways in which text and images surround children in the twenty-first century. In this process we also look closely at our own daily lives and the lives of children and families in our

spaces and beyond. As we do this, one thing that increasingly stands out is the way in which children notice and mimic the literacy habits of surrounding adults. They are extremely aware of the ways in which adults use multimedia tools to communicate information in the world.

Innovating Play Bonus Resources:
Find more at innovatingplay.world/kmail

From a very early age children are exposed to and begin to read images through logos, icons, and avatars. They see communication through texting, messaging apps, and email. Interacting with print and images has become more prevalent in our lives than perhaps ever before. Therefore it is our responsibility to offer opportunities to mirror these experiences in the classroom for young children. We need to seek new ways to safely and effectively expose them to letters, words, and images so that they can transfer their understanding of literacy in a way that makes sense in their world.

It is with this mindset that Kid Mail, or Kmail, was created. As kindergarten teachers, we wanted to offer children a way to communicate using letters, words, sentences, and images to transfer thoughts and ideas in ways that reflect what they see happening every day. We also knew that, as part of this experience, we needed to be mindful of helping children begin to understand *how* to communicate within this form.

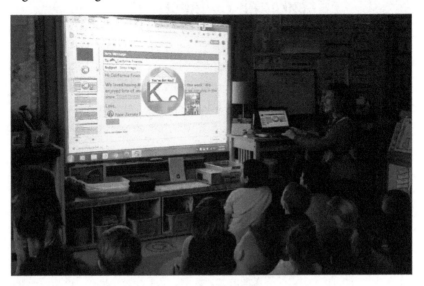

Innovating Play Bonus Resources: Find more at innovatingplay.world/customizekmail

Kmail is created and shared through Google Slides and is meant to be a social experience involving both the teachers and the students. It is a think-aloud, which provides the opportunity to model very directly and explicitly what happens in the heads of readers and writers when we communicate in any format, but in this case specifically using a digital format.[5] Kmail is also a safe way to expose children to authentic writing experiences that are connected to their everyday lives and observations. The key is not just in the digital piece, but in the sharing, thinking aloud, and modeling as the instruction is happening. In other words, for the Kmail experience to be most meaningful, it requires clear and focused instruction, just as with any other literacy experience.

---

5   Teachers use a think-aloud strategy to verbalize and model for students in order to demonstrate comprehension, problem-solving, and practical ways to process information.

Explore Author's Purpose through Collaboration

Many of our Extended Reading experiences allowed for our classes to connect and learn together in some form. As our year together progressed we began to wonder more specifically about how to nurture depth in collaboration. What does deep collaboration look like for any group of learners, but more specifically, what would it look like with young children? How could we create an experience that would allow for meaningful collaboration in which students were accountable for communicating and contributing? These questions brought us to the idea of building and exploring a collaborative literacy Extended Reading approach.

A Kindness Book From New Jersey		
Book	**Message**	**Promise**
It Takes a Village (Hillary Rodham Clinton)	• Be kind to everyone and have peace and love. • Helping is caring. • Build together. • Be respectful to everyone.	We use teamwork.

As Martin Luther King Jr. would be recognized and celebrated during the month of January, we saw the opportunity to build on the idea of kindness as our connection point. We started by selecting five books with clear messages of caring and kindness that our students could explore. We then set up collaborative Google Slides in order to help us facilitate this experience for the kids. Instead of having each class read and do the work for all of the books, we divided the texts between the classes.

As part of this experience, children in each class knew that they were responsible for communicating the ideas in their assigned books clearly to the other class. This sense of accountability and ownership was a game changer. Suddenly they were not completing their learning task solely for themselves or because the teacher said so; their contribution mattered because the other class was counting on them to follow through. In this safe way, we planted seeds for what it means to collaborate. We helped them to feel the value of their contributions and the ways in which their actions within a collaboration impact everyone involved.

Collaborative opportunities are often saved for older grades as children learn the sometimes-frustrating lessons of working together in both digital and physical spaces. Without the context and seeds planted early, students may struggle to see the ways in which their participation in a collaboration will impact themselves, others, and the group as a whole. Students may be left feeling defeated or lacking a sense of their own value, as some members may take on a heavy workload while others may participate minimally. This twenty-first-century skill is so critical that it is part of just about every job that children may consider someday. Instead of waiting until later to allow children to see the benefit and impact of collaboration, we can empower young children to let it become part of what they know, feel, and value in their interactions with others.

As we worked within the shared Google Slides each day over the course of the week, both classes contributed by listening to their selected story, identifying the author's purpose as the teacher recorded their words on the slide, and working together to articulate a sentence to add to a kindness promise that the classes would make to each other. The kindness promise would become a mission statement that would be built together, upheld by both classes, and express the values that we shared in physical and virtual spaces. It was in the process of creating the kindness promise and the mission statement that our children felt the words moving beyond the book. They not only identified the author's purpose in each story, they saw the ways in which that purpose was put into action through their collaboration.

As with all our collaborative projects, we provide a balance of experiences to support learning connections. For example, our students traced and decorated their handprints, which we would later use to decorate a print-out of our kindness promise. As they completed this activity during Connected Play (see Chapter 7), they reflected on their collaborative experience with the books and Google Slides. Their conversations with each other reflected the messages from the book as they shared, respectfully questioned, complimented, and supported each other. They carefully and thoughtfully decorated handprints (one for each hand) that would represent their contribution to both classes. Then each child selected one handprint to be placed around the kindness promise in their classroom, while the other would be mailed to the collaborating classroom on the other side of the country. Through this activity, children saw the ways in which their worlds were connected and woven together. Beyond this, they also saw how words and actions are meant to move beyond the book and beyond the screen, to influence how we live and nurture each other each day.

Innovating Play Bonus Resources: Find more at
innovatingplay.world/kindness
innovatingplay.world/promiseslides
innovatingplay.world/kindnesswriting

Extended Learning Experience with Families

We love to invite families into classroom experiences by creating a digital space that weaves learning together. One of the ways we do this is by taking advantage of the slides that we use during a week for facilitating learning. In this section we are going to show you how we used our facilitation slides and included documentation pieces to share the experience that took place when studying the nursery rhyme "Pat-a-Cake."

In order to efficiently create a space to share with families, we set up a separate Google Slide deck, which we published to the web. In the first slide we invited families to explore the nursery rhyme we were studying. We intentionally began by including a video that we had used during our in-class Extended Reading experience. Just as we establish the point of connection with the children in the classroom, it is helpful to make this introduction clear and specific for families as they consider the week of learning experiences as a whole.

We know that families wonder how their children are learning and what their day looks like in the classroom. Caregivers will often ask questions about how their child is progressing as a reader and what they can do to support further growth at home. Sharing experiences that are connected to the Extended Reading lessons creates opportunities for caregivers to follow up at home. The next image is a slide where we shared a copy of the nursery rhyme and videos of key sight words the children were to practice. We simply copied this slide from our collection of weekly slides into the sharing space. Extending learning to families does not have to look like traditional homework. In fact we love the idea of replacing traditional homework with meaningful experiences that can be enjoyed by families together; one way to do this is to heed our students' frequent requests to share materials and activities with their families so they can "play at home."

Creating a class book is a great way to retell stories. Therefore, we create class book templates in Google Slides for printing hands-on classroom books. The benefit of creating the print book in Google Slides is that those same images can then be moved to the shared slide deck so children and their families can view a digital version of the book at home.

Unlike the printed class book that stays in our classroom library, our digital class book will often include additional elements to build a comprehensive view of the experience. In Google Slides you can use a single slide to create a collage of the experience. Including photos of students helps to capture the process, allows parents to see the experience as a whole, and provides conversation starters at home. This means that before families read the children's final product, they can see them engaged in its creation, offering a window into classroom life.

To replicate the actual class book, we added photos of children's writing to slides to create the digital version of our class book. While this book provides a tactile experience in the classroom (including raised foam letters that support a multisensory approach to alphabet letters and sounds), the digital version can be enjoyed anywhere and used to support reading engagement outside of school.

We like to conclude our family sharing slide deck by offering the purpose and intentions behind the learning experience as a whole. Sharing objectives and goals for the Extended Reading experiences helps families to see the bigger picture of learning. Using this slide to

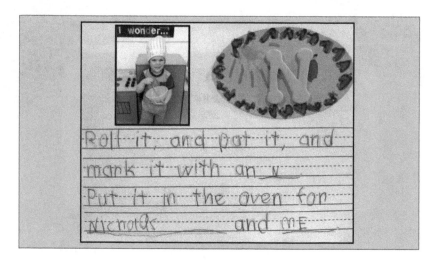

share a classroom resource and optional follow-up experiences students can have at home empowers families to learn together. In this example, we provide a way for families to transfer literacy directly into the home. Caregivers are given a special role and a voice in helping their children to transfer classroom lessons into the real world.

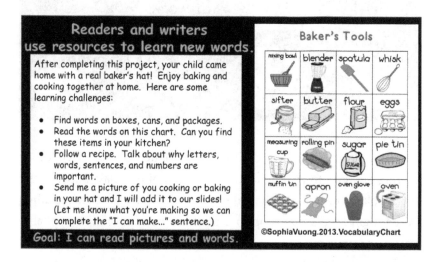

One of the perks of Google Slides is the ability to add as many slides as you need—meaning you can always create space for learning to continue. Children enjoy seeing their peers learn at home, so we used Seesaw to invite families to share photos and encourage them to use the available Seesaw tools to show their learning at home. As families shared photos from this experience, we added these images to our slides and revisited them during the school day. As children saw what was happening with their peers, inspiration to participate increased. Children reestablished their connection to the learning and began to wonder, "Can I do that at home too?" Many would excitedly return the next day to share with us that they had played at home, too, and were excited for their moment to share their learning discoveries with their peers.

Throughout this process, we remain sensitive to the variety of family situations that may impact children's level of participation outside the classroom. For this reason we also continuously acknowledge that, just as classrooms are different, families work differently as well. We assure children that various opportunities to participate in a variety of ways will be presented during our year together. We also attempt to set up a variety of extension opportunities to connect learning through play in the classroom. In this example, children who may not have had the chance to participate in a follow-up baking activity at home had the option of visiting the dramatic play area during Community Play where baking props were available to connect learning in special ways.

As we noted earlier, publishing the slides to the web (a feature within Google Slides) creates a hyperlink that makes it easy to share them with families. We shared the published link in Seesaw with a caption inviting families to join the fun. The comment feature in Seesaw allows others to acknowledge and celebrate the efforts of the class and helps students feel connected to a broad community of learners.

While in this specific family extension we documented an individual classroom experience, the Innovating Play Cycle exists within its development. When creating a family extension for Extended Reading, we go through each part of the cycle:

Connect

Extended Reading means that the idea of literacy lives beyond the book and represents creative and meaningful multimedia experiences along with printed text. We establish the connection between home and school as we document and invite families to be a part of learning.

Good morning friends and families! We had so much fun exploring our nursery rhyme this week! Click this link to take a closer look at our amazing kindergartners and find lots of ways to keep playing and learning at home.

Wonder

Extended Reading offers us new ways to explore how we can bring meaningful literacy experiences into the homes of our students. We continuously ask: What parts of this experience will help families feel included in the process and products of learning? What are the goals and objectives that we want to make clear to families? How can we invite families to extend learning at home and share back with the class?

Play

Children naturally seek playful experiences in school and at home. Offering families ways to continue to weave together learning and play supports seamless transfer of knowledge. It also supports healthy overall development for young children as we encourage balanced and meaningful play at home. We have had many families thank us for the guidance, direction, and support that our family sharing pieces offer in their everyday lives.

Discover

One of the most powerful gifts we can offer caregivers is the opportunity to truly discover their child as a learner. By creating a window into the classroom, offering visual documentation, and providing specific direction for families, we strengthen the bond that families feel with their child as a learner. This supports communication between the caregiver and the child and provides important common ground for teachers and families as they share, problem-solve, and move through the year together.

Learning with the #InnovatingPlay Community

How do you take a reading experience
beyond the text of a book?

innovatingplay.world/bookq4

Science

As districts across the United States navigate Next Generation Science Standards, educators across grade levels are reaching for resources and experiences that provide authentic opportunities to develop depth in scientific thinking. It is no longer enough for students to consume and demonstrate understanding of information within isolated experiences; today, they are being asked to communicate, collaborate, inquire, problem-solve, and think with flexibility as they design, explore, and discover. As teachers of young children we are keenly aware of the importance of using hands-on investigation to observe and discover scientific principles as they naturally exist in the world. When we consider the role of technology in young children's education, we are mindful to protect this foundation. We would never substitute these essential experiences with technology, but we are always open to using new tools to expand, enrich, and create broader context for understanding. In this chapter we will share some specific examples of ways that we use technology to redefine traditional practices in order to explore scientific concepts through joyful creation and interaction.

One of the key elements in broadening children's understanding of scientific concepts is helping them take what is observable in front of them and apply it to their understanding of the larger world. While we can expand children's views of the world in a variety of ways using premade resources such as books or videos, we set out to explore the unique possibilities that our classroom collaboration presented in this area. We wondered how we could use our collaboration across the country to support deeper understanding of concepts by allowing the children to be communicators and creators in their experiences together. In this chapter we will explore daily practices for sharing between our classrooms as well as special projects that we facilitated to explore science standards in ways that generate depth of understanding along with meaningful connection and creation.

Transforming the Weather Reporting Ritual

Many teachers in primary grades have a weather reporting ritual. They might provide a place to indicate the weather on a classroom calendar, a weather wheel, or a chart to graph the weather. During Christine's first year of teaching, her class sang a weather song as the child designated as the weather reporter popped his or her head out the door to see what the weather was outside. The class then graphed the reporter's observation in a chart in Google Sheets, and that was it for the weather ritual.

Since Christine is located in Southern California, the weather is usually partly sunny or sunny. With such consistent weather, you can imagine how similar those monthly graphs looked! Meanwhile, Jessica was on the other side of the country in New Jersey creating a similar style of weather graph with her class on chart paper. Data varied from month to month, as seasonal changes meant vast weather shifts throughout the year. Weather information was interesting when considered over time, but the routine often became simply another activity that they checked off the list for the day.

Fast-forward to the next school year, when we started collaborating. As we explored working together, a big question that kept coming up was how to create an ongoing collaboration between our classes. We each saw the potential to redefine global collaboration to mean more than just a few isolated experiences between classes. We felt compelled to find out what would happen if we could create a way for our classes to see, hear, and connect with each other *every single school day.*

Because the weather reporting ritual was something both of our classes did, we quickly recognized the potential for this to form the roots of a daily collaboration.

With the aim of letting children see, hear, and participate in the weather reporting experience, we set up a Flipgrid in order to record and share the weather daily. By including a video of a weather song, we created a shared experience between classes, as they would both sing the same song to begin the weather ritual for the day. Children in New Jersey would observe the weather locally and get to see the weather report from the day before in California. (Children developed a broader concept of the world as they saw the impact of time differences, just as they did during the Wish You Well ritual). In California, children would be able to observe their own local weather as well as the same-day weather report from New Jersey. Suddenly the kids had the opportunity to peek into each other's worlds on a daily basis.

In the example shown here, we share a view of the weather experience as children would see it projected in the classroom. Similar to the Morning Message routine, including the weather song directly in Flipgrid allowed for efficient flow of instruction as we began by singing this song each day. Details such as shared songs add to the special common language and culture developed between the classrooms. As this song is a staple kindergarten favorite each year, it has been a consistent part of our weather collaboration from the beginning. (In our third year of collaborating, we were thrilled to connect with the song creator, Nancy Kopman, who did a special weather report from Canada, which we were able to add to our Flipgrid. We pinned her response to the beginning of the grid, and children often requested to hear her weather report again as a special treat.) Some other details to note in this example:

- Students have the class job as the weather reporter for an entire week. Children are often excited to see who their weather buddy is in the other class, and they enjoy getting to know that friend as the week progresses.

- In the name and title section of each video we usually put the student's name (replaced here with teacher names), along with a few words describing the weather including temperature or other special notes about the day.
- The small circles on a video represent responses to that specific weather report. While we do not use the response option daily, we do use this feature to communicate questions, ideas, observations, and follow-up messages to each other when appropriate.

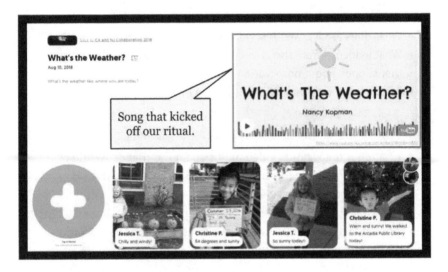

The simple addition of this format extended the traditional weather reporting experience in so many ways. Learning became magical as we were able to see each other's spaces. We had the opportunity to reply to the weather report video and ask questions between classrooms. Our collaboration gave us an opportunity to ask deeper questions that allowed children to compare, contrast, and closely examine the details of weather observations. Weather reporting time often inspired unique learning experiences, leading to an emergent curriculum developed between teachers and students in both classrooms.[1]

---

1   An emergent curriculum focuses on planning, analyzing, and observing the interests, ideas, and thoughts of the children in order to guide instruction.

Facilitation Questions for Weather Reporting

TRADITIONAL WEATHER CHECK

- What do you notice about the weather when you look out the window?

ENHANCED BY VIDEO-RECORDING THE WEATHER REPORT

- What does today's weather video tell us about today's weather?
- What evidence from the environment do you notice in the video that supports your observation?
- What are we wearing? Why is it important?

TRANSFORMED BY COLLABORATING WITH ANOTHER CLASS

- What does the weather video tell us about our friends' weather? What evidence from the environment do you notice in the video that supports your observation?
- What was their weather reporter wearing? Why is that important?
- What are we wearing? How is it the same or different?
- Why is it important to observe weather in different places in the world?
- What if all weather was the same?

We both saw value in the graphing component of our previous weather rituals and decided to create a space where our classes could have access to each other's weather data. The Duo Weather Template includes a space for two graphs to be viewed side by side. After viewing the weather reports on Flipgrid, the weather reporter uses the computer to fill in the type of weather for the day. The spreadsheet is conditionally formatted so that when any text is typed in a cell in the graph, the cell changes color. Weather is graphed daily, with each month in its own sheet within the same file.

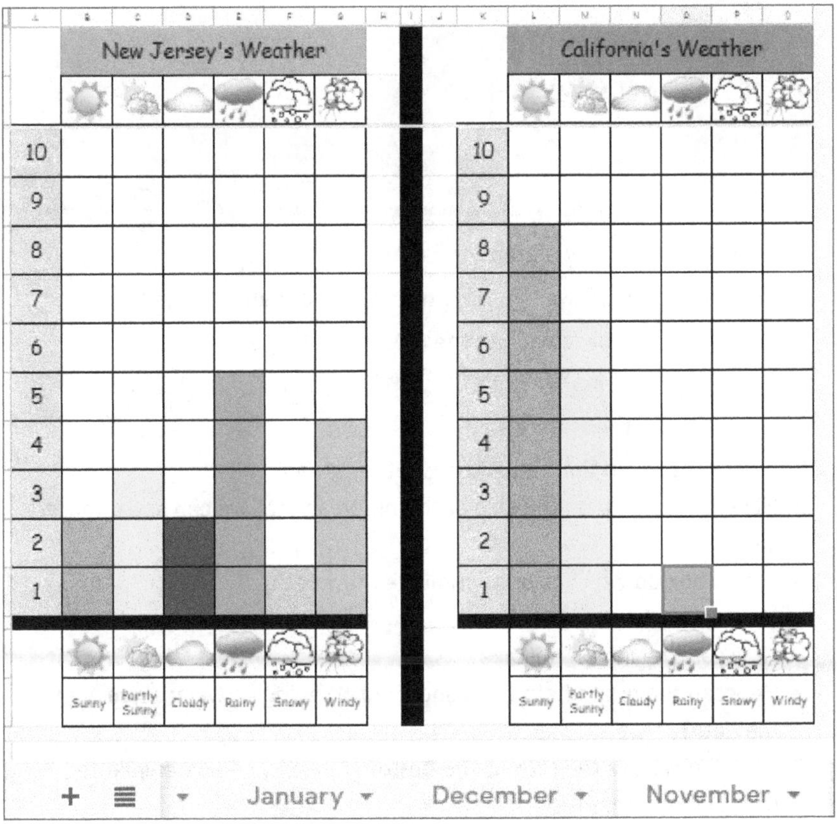

	New Jersey's Weather									California's Weather					

New Jersey's Weather

	Sunny	Partly Sunny	Cloudy	Rainy	Snowy	Windy

California's Weather

	Sunny	Partly Sunny	Cloudy	Rainy	Snowy	Windy

+ ≡ ▼   January ▼   December ▼   November ▼

Creating shared access to our graphs in Google Sheets invites children to think critically as they count, compare, and analyze weather types on a daily basis. Discussions can go further when taking into account the location of our spaces geographically and the impact of seasonal changes that are (or are not) taking place. A number of facilitation questions can be asked to provoke meaningful, in-depth conversation.

Innovating Play Bonus Resources: Find more at
innovatingplay.world/weathergraph
innovatingplay.world/duoweather
innovatingplay.world/weatherflipgrid

Facilitation Questions for Weather Graphing

TRADITIONAL ON CHART PAPER

- What weather will we graph today?
- How many more/fewer ___ days have we had than ___ days?
- Which weather have we had the most/least?

ENHANCED BY GRAPHING GOOGLE SHEETS

- Where is the tab that holds the weather graph?
- How can we change the size of the graph so that we can see it more clearly?
- Which box do we click on to indicate the weather?
- How do we fill the box?
- How can we undo a mistake?
- How can the graph help us to show our thinking as we analyze the data?
- How can we use the tabs at the bottom to easily compare weather between months?

TRANSFORMED BY COLLABORATING WITH ANOTHER CLASS

- What observations can you make about the weather graphs?
- How many more/fewer ___ days has New Jersey had than California?
- How many more ___ days would New Jersey need to equal California's ___ days?
- Do you notice more similar/different weather this month between California and New Jersey? Why?
- How do the seasonal changes impact the weather in New Jersey and California? Are they the same or different? Which months have had the most similarities? Which months have had the most differences?
- Why is it important to notice what is the same and different in our weather graphs?
- How can comparing weather graphs help people?

Whether you decide to create a new digital space for weather reporting and graphing routines or decide to explore a collaborative experience together, we encourage you to consider the following suggestions to reframe your facilitation of routines:

- **Use the Google Sheets Template to set up a class weather graph.** Consider what elements of your routine you would like to continue as you shift to a digital space. Think about how you would like to facilitate and encourage natural exploration of tools within this space.
- **Set up a weather Flipgrid for daily recording.** Even if you are creating a Flipgrid to be used within one space, consider the ways that recording around your school can change your students' perspective of their immediate world.
- **Be ready to capture the sky, plant growth, and evidence of the impact of weather on the environment.** Videos give you the chance to document specific weather observations and seasonal changes. We loved recording by the school garden, and Jessica kept black paper in the freezer to catch snowflakes that could then be viewed on video.
- **Consider a routine for recording weather videos that works with your schedule.** We each designated the "weather reporter" as a weekly job for students and had a specific time that worked for recording. Taking a few minutes of recess time for the teacher and the weather reporter to record the weather works well and creates the opportunity for special one-on-one teachable moments.
- **Scaffold the weather reporting experience.** Weather videos present a wonderful opportunity for students to practice speaking in complete sentences, articulating their words, moderating their volume, and expressing themselves. When watching weather reports, support children in recognizing the efforts and growth of their peers as speakers and communicators.

Playing in the Forest

After we set up our class connection through daily weather reports, we noticed how much there was that children would see, hear, and wonder about. They began to ask questions about the environment of the other school. They noticed details such as sound, color, and plant life. They spontaneously pointed out amazing similarities and vast differences. The multimedia weather report was our window into the daily authentic experiences of children separated by 2,500 miles. This window would provide a deep meaningful look at how these similarities and differences moved beyond humans and impacted plants, animals, and the surrounding environments as well. It gave us the opportunity to address the Next Generation Science Standards through experiences that we would build and create between our classes.

As children observed the ways in which seasonal changes impacted trees and plant life in both New Jersey and California, they began to wonder how this phenomenon impacts other things in the environment, such as animals. We decided to use this curiosity as an opportunity to help children look more deeply at the impact of seasonal changes on environments, including their effects on plants, animals, and people. The breakdown of this experience can be found in our lesson plan format described in the opening of Part Two and spelled out in the following pages.

Once our weather routine was established, students soon started making observations about the environments surrounding both of our schools. A couple of months in, while weather reports from Southern California continued to show sunshine and warm weather, weather reports from the same days reflected that children in New Jersey were beginning to layer clothing, and trees were changing colors. In each of our classrooms, we began to plant seeds for our exploration by accessing resources and integrating them into instruction throughout the day. Both classes had access to Reading A-Z and YouTube videos that would create common background knowledge between the classes.

CONNECT

Guiding Questions

- What is the connecting piece, the tie, that is bringing you together?
- What concepts or ideas help kids bridge previous learning/experiences to the next set of concepts and ideas?

Previous Discoveries/Connections

Kids have been learning about trees, parts of the tree, how trees grow, and seasonal changes.

Weather reports have allowed children in California to see the changes to the trees in New Jersey. California trees are just starting to show signs of changes.

Bridging Pieces—Trees to Forest Animals

New Jersey
Our leaves are changing!

- What is it called when groups of trees grow in the same space? (Forest) Use this connection to spark curiosity about what animals live in the forest.
- "Forest Habitat" video from YouTube
- *The Forest*—Reading A-Z book
- Be sure to collect connections being built and any questions!

Learning Objectives: What goals do the classes share that need to be worked on?

Common Core State Standards—English Language Arts

Writing:

- Use a combination of drawing, dictating, and writing to compose informative/explanatory texts in which they name what they are writing about and supply some information about the topic. (W.K.2)
- Participate in shared research and writing projects. (W.K.7)
- With guidance and support from adults, recall information from experiences or gather information from provided sources to answer a question. (W.K.8)

Speaking and Listening:

Speak audibly and express thoughts, feelings, and ideas clearly. (SL.K.6)

Next Generation Science Standards Cross-Cutting Concepts:

Systems and System Models

- Systems in the natural and designed world have parts that work together. (K-ESS2-2), (K-ESS3-1)

Disciplinary Core Ideas:

Organization for Matter and Energy Flow in Organisms (LS1.C)

- All animals need food in order to live and grow. They obtain their food from plants or from other animals. Plants need water and light to live and grow. (K-LS1-1)

Biogeology (ESS2.E)

- Plants and animals can change their environment. (K-ESS2-2)

Natural Resources (ESS3.A)

- Living things need water, air, and resources from the land, and they live in places that have the things they need. Humans use natural resources for everything they do. (K-ESS3-1)

Science and Engineering Practices:

Developing and Using Models

- Modeling in K–2 builds on prior experiences and progresses to include using and developing models (i.e., diagram, drawing, physical replica, diorama, dramatization, storyboard) that represent concrete events or design solutions.
- Use a model to represent relationships in the natural world. (K-ESS3-1)

Technology

ISTE Standards for Students

- Global Collaborator - 7b Students use digital tools to connect with learners from a variety of backgrounds and cultures, engaging with them in ways that broaden mutual understanding and learning.
- Creative Communicator - 6c Students communicate complex ideas clearly and effectively by creating or using a variety of digital objects such as visualizations, models, or simulations.

New Jersey Core Curriculum Content Standards—Technology

- Demonstrate developmentally appropriate navigation skills in virtual environments. (8.1.2.A.4)

- Students use digital media and environments to communicate and work collaboratively, including at a distance, to support individual learning and contribute to the learning of others. (8.1.2.C)
- Communicate information and ideas to multiple audiences using a variety of media and formats. (8.1.2.C.CS2)
- Develop cultural understanding and global awareness by engaging with learners of other cultures. (8.1.2.C.CS3)
- Engage in a variety of developmentally appropriate learning activities with students in other classes, schools, or countries using various media formats such as online collaborative tools and social media. (8.1.2.C.1)

This connection inspired rich discussions in which the children pondered what other changes might be happening if the trees were changing color. How would these changes impact other plants, animals, and people? We used these questions to continue to weave literacy and science standards together as our experience continued to unfold.

Innovating Play Bonus Resources: Find more at innovatingplay.world/forestexploring innovatingplay.world/forestlittlebook

We knew it was important to set up a space for a collaborative project that captured the current questions of the children and continue to build a sense of curiosity. As teachers we worked together in a shared Google Slide deck to create space to delve into children's curiosity and begin to develop ideas for exploration and play. When slides were completed, each of us made a copy so that the individual classes had their own space to capture their ideas.

WONDER

Guiding Questions:

- How will you create curiosity?
- How are you going to capture the kids' questions?

Resources and Ideas:

- Adventures in the Forest slides include pictures and videos of animals from the forest.
- The wonder box on the second slide allows children to extend what they hear in the forest habitat video and begin to connect with their own curiosity.
- After the kids venture through the forest (clicking on animals in the first slide that are hyperlinked to individual slides with informational videos) they can choose an animal to wonder and learn more about.
- What animal do you want to learn more about? What about that animal do you want to know?

Week I: Research and Organizing Information

Each class worked through these slides over the course of the week. Students had the chance to watch the corresponding video for each forest animal and identify specific facts. While the teacher recorded those facts on the discovery space provided in the slides, each child also had a copy of the little book in which they independently recorded data and observations as the teacher modeled on the projected slide. The little book was designed so that young readers and writers would have a way to visually organize and analyze information as it applied to each animal. This would support comparing and contrasting the needs and characteristics of each animal type individually and as they relate to each other.

Weeks 2–3: Drawing, Synthesizing, and Recording Information

To continue to play with their learning, children were later given a choice of forest animals to learn to draw by using selected drawing videos that were included in the Adventures in the Forest slides. Students continued to solidify their understanding as they noticed the details of the animals. They made connections to the information they had learned about animal characteristics and survival within the forest habitat. Once drawings were completed, children came together to share their drawings and an interesting fact about their chosen animal. Teachers collected the animal drawings to be used later to create two different forest models that would represent the forest as a system. The first model would be a classroom mural, and the second would be a digital version shared between classes. To prepare for the digital version, teachers removed the background from each child's drawing and saved the drawings as PNG images.

In order to bring classes together once again, we created a shared forest Flipgrid with a topic for each animal. Children from both classes recorded one fact that they had learned about their chosen animal under the appropriate topic. This allowed us to create a space for all children to feel represented and have a voice in the culminating project that would reflect their learning back and support the learning of peers.

Weeks 4–5: Creation and Exploration

The creation of the two murals brought us to the final stages of this project. While the classroom mural represented a more traditional display, the digital mural offered an interactive representation that would allow learning to continue. To build the digital mural, we used the same forest animal image that began the Adventures in the Forest slides. What we approached differently was the use of hyperlinks for animals on the title slide. In this version, the link would bring students to a new slide that showed all of their drawings of the same animal together. For example, clicking on the fox image on the title slide would bring you to the slide containing drawings of all of the foxes from both classes. To add an extra-special detail to this, each individual animal drawing could be hyperlinked to a slide that contained the informational video we had downloaded from Flipgrid. This digital mural made for a wonderful learning center that kids could explore independently. Having the physical classroom mural and the digital mural offered multiple ways of visualizing and integrating knowledge of the forest as a system.

PLAY

Guiding Questions:
• How and where will the experience(s) be facilitated?

Activities
Continuing in the Adventures in the Forest slides, the class studies one animal each day by watching the animal video and listening for information to share in the discoveries section.

Children record information in a little book.

As a class, record information on the graph used for analyzing and comparing animals.

✔️	Diurnal ☀️	Nocturnal 🌙	In/On a Tree 🌳	Near a Tree 🌳	Gets Food From Plants	Gets Food From Animals
🦌						
🦉						
🦝						
🐻						
🦊						
🐾						

After studying all of the animals as a class, children choose one animal to draw using a guided drawing video.

Based on the animal the children draw, they choose one fact about that animal to record on video. (Flipgrid is a nice space to host all the videos.)

CA Friend
A girl moose is called a cow.

NJ Friend
Moose only eat plants.

A model of the forest as a system is created in the classroom to show information learned by the children along with their drawings next to a classroom tree. A language experience chart, which is posted alongside the system display, is used for children's discoveries so they can see their oral language translated into print.

A digital mural is created between classes and includes children's animal drawings. If creating in Google Slides, each child's video may be included on its own slide and hyperlinked to the child's respective animal drawing.

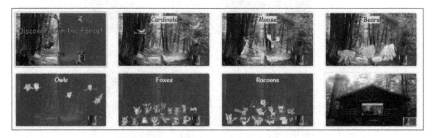

Week 6: Reflection and Discovery

As this project came to a close, final discoveries were explored by looking at an image of both schools using a bird's-eye view from Google Maps. Children noted the difference in the scene from above, specifically the abundance of trees around the school in New Jersey and the lack of trees around the school in California. This helped them to draw conclusions about plant and animal life as it could be found in each space. Bringing our classes together for this study offered a broad view of the scientific concepts they had explored and how those concepts relate to familiar spaces near and far.

DISCOVER

Guiding Question:

- What tools will you use for documentation and reflection, and how will you use them?

Ideas:

- Discovery space, labeled "Our Discoveries," in the Adventures in the Forest slides allows children to process and share information about each animal.

- Classroom model (bulletin board display) gives children a visual for processing and reflecting on their learning.

- Digital mural (in the photographs below) empowers children to be teachers and learners because their animal drawing/video fact is included and they get to tune in to the animal facts of their peers.

- The bird's-eye view (screenshot images from Google Maps) of our schools shows the surrounding areas, allowing children to make connections about why animals may or may not be seen in and around their homes.

Reflection Questions	
How do plants and animals work together? What do you know about animals in each of our spaces by looking carefully at these pictures?	 

This experience took place over the course of a little over a month to allow children to fully engage in each part of the Innovating Play Cycle within and between classes. The integration of technology served to connect children and allowed for meaningful conceptualization of scientific knowledge as it applied to understanding local surroundings and the surroundings of the collaborating class in a different space.

Playing at the Farm

Once we knew the possibilities for exploring and using physical and digital spaces, we were on the lookout for more opportunities to play. Throughout our first two years of collaboration we had many opportunities to compare and contrast our surroundings. As we moved forward we found opportunities to personalize experiences further so that they truly reflected the connection, wonder, play, and discoveries of our students.

Innovating Play Bonus Resources: Find more at
innovatingplay.world/farmexploring
innovatingplay.world/wonderbubble
innovatingplay.world/farmanimalinfo
innovatingplay.world/farmplayingsample

One special opportunity for this type of personalization through technology came when we embarked on a study of farm animals together. Through late winter and early spring weather reports and experiences, children had come to understand that plant life was flourishing in California while the ground was just beginning to thaw in New Jersey. California friends had helped the children in New Jersey explore their school garden, and this caused us to wonder about what else we could share that might be different. Although the weather supported plant life in California, there were other elements of the environment that impacted their resources. There are no local farms accessible to Christine's kids in the part of California where they live. On the other hand, Jessica's school is located in a more rural setting, so she and her kids embraced the chance to share something that is local and easily accessible to them. Again, we began by using common resources available to both classes to incorporate background knowledge and encourage further curiosity about life on the farm.

CONNECT

Guiding Questions:
- What is the connecting piece, the tie, that is bringing you together?
- What concepts or ideas help kids bridge previous learning/experiences to the next set of concepts and ideas?

Previous Discoveries/Connections:
- Kids learned about plant life in the garden and what the garden has to offer.
- Kids recalled their exploration experiences...
- ...when kids in California saw New Jersey and how bare it was in the winter compared to their garden via a weather report.
- ...in the garden when the California children toured their garden and shared the experience with their New Jersey friends via a weather report.
- ...when the California children went back to the garden to do some planting and observe plants, and brought their New Jersey friends along via Google Hangouts.

February in New Jersey   February in California

Bridging Pieces—Garden to Farm
- Resurface some wonders/discoveries that were made during the garden experience.

- Facilitate discussion on the essential question: Where else do you get food? This leads to how stores, restaurants, etc. get their supply of food.
- "Sesame Street: Big Bird Visits A Farm" video on YouTube
- *The Food We Eat* — Reading A-Z book
- Be sure to collect connections being built and any questions!

Learning Objectives: What goals do the classes share that need to be worked on?

Common Core State Standards — English Language Arts

Writing

- Use a combination of drawing, dictating, and writing to compose informative/explanatory texts in which they name what they are writing about and supply some information about the topic. (W.K.2)
- Participate in shared research and writing projects. (W.K.7)
- With guidance and support from adults, recall information from experiences or gather information from provided sources to answer a question. (W.K.8)

Speaking and Listening

- Add drawings or other visual displays to descriptions as desired to provide additional detail. (SL.K.5)
- Speak audibly and express thoughts, feelings, and ideas clearly. (SL.K.6)
- Next Generation Science Standards
- Use observations to describe patterns of what plants and animals (including humans) need to survive. (K-LS1-1)

Technology

ISTE Standards for Students

- Global Collaborator - 7b Students use digital tools to connect with learners from a variety of backgrounds and cultures, engaging with them in ways that broaden mutual understanding and learning.

New Jersey Core Curriculum Content Standards — Technology

- Demonstrate developmentally appropriate navigation skills in virtual environments. (8.1.2.A.4)

- Students use digital media and environments to communicate and work collaboratively, including at a distance, to support individual learning and contribute to the learning of others. (8.1.2.C)
- Communicate information and ideas to multiple audiences using a variety of media and formats. (8.1.2.C.CS2)
- Develop cultural understanding and global awareness by engaging with learners of other cultures. (8.1.2.C.CS3)
- Engage in a variety of developmentally appropriate learning activities with students in other classes, schools, or countries using various media formats such as online collaborative tools and social media. (8.1.2.C.1)

Week 1: Teacher Preparation and Creating Space for Wonder

To start off the experience, Jessica visited a few local farms and collected images and videos of animals and their living spaces. We took those pieces and created a virtual farm experience so the kids could explore the farm together. We began by creating Google Slides that would serve to kick off the virtual farm experience for the kids. Similar to the forest project, animal images on the first slide were hyperlinked to images and videos on a corresponding slide. This time, those images and videos would come directly from the farms in New Jersey. This created excitement for the children in Jessica's class as they saw familiar animals and settings appear on the screen. Christine's students, on the other hand, would experience the excitement of visiting another place close to their buddy class that they had come to know so well.

Week 2: Exploring Ideas and Capturing Student Choice

The virtual farm experience created an opportunity for the kids to think of an animal they would like to learn more about. In Christine's class, students used special paper to draw and write about their chosen farm animal. In Jessica's class, the children had the opportunity to use video recording in Seesaw to capture and share their curiosity with their families. Instead of sharing the end product in isolation, families were brought in each step of the way as children moved through the process.

WONDER

Guiding Questions:

- How will you create wonder?
- How are you going to capture the kids' questions?

Resources and Ideas:

- Adventures at the Farm slides presentation—includes pictures and videos of animals from local farms in New Jersey.

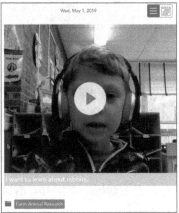

- After exploring the farm, children choose an animal to wonder and learn more about.

- What animal do you want to learn more about? What about that animal do you want to know?

- I Wonder Thought Cloud/Mental Image—kids draw a picture of their mental image and write a sentence to support their wonder.

- Kids use the Seesaw video tool to talk about the animal they chose and explain their choice. Videos are shared with families.

Week 3: Researching, Drawing, and Recording

To allow children to explore their chosen animal independently, we created a set of Google Slides with informational videos, along with a drawing video. The kids took notes independently this time and drew their animal. Once the children completed their research, teachers recorded individual videos of students sharing a fact about their animal. Instead of using Flipgrid, Jessica chose to record her videos directly into Seesaw so that families would see their child's research. This helped to bridge the connection for families between the animal their child had wondered about and selected and what they had learned through their research. Again, similar to the forest project, these videos would be used to contribute to an interactive digital mural created by and shared between our two classes.

Weeks 4-5: Putting It All Together

The final mural was completed by removing backgrounds from the animal drawings and inserting the drawings into appropriate backgrounds in slides. Ducks swam in the pond, sheep and cows grazed in the fields, and pigs wallowed in the mud. Animal pictures drawn by each student were then hyperlinked to a slide with the individual video of the creator sharing the fact about their animal.

–––––––––––––––––––––––– PLAY ––––––––––––––––––

Guiding Questions:
- How and where will the experience(s) be facilitated?

Activities:
- Kids conduct research and take notes on their chosen animal by referencing a Google Doc list of the farm animals (links will lead to Google Slides presentations for each animal).

Links to Hyper Slides for Research
horses
cows
goats

- Kids will draw their animal using a guided drawing video.
- Kids choose one fact to record.

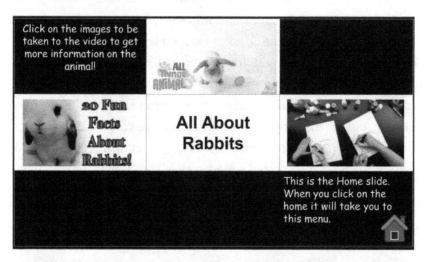

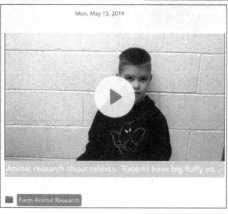

Week 6: Teaching Each Other

This project made a fantastic kid-created learning center once the digital mural was completed. While they became experts on the animal of their choice, students from both classes were able to share their learning in order to create the bigger picture of animal life on a farm as part of a larger system. Final projects such as this one allow children to be creators and teachers in their learning process. We love using these projects for the Technology and Communication center during Connected Play (discussed in further detail in Chapter 7).

DISCOVER

Guiding Question:
- What tools will you use for documentation and reflection, and how will you use them?

Playing at the Farm collaborative slides:
- Kids get to be teachers and learners because their animal drawing and video fact are included, and they get to tune in to the animal facts of their peers.

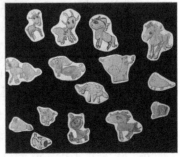

The Pumpkin Patch:
Exploring the World Together

When we think about connection points for learning, we need to consider the vast array of possibilities available to us. In the past we were limited to the resources or experiences we could create within the walls of the classroom in order to provide a sense of connection. While there are many wonderful ways to continue to provide these types of experiences, we are lucky to live in a time where we can dream bigger and bring those dreams to life. In this section we invite you to join us on our journey through a physical and virtual field trip that was experienced, created, and facilitated with our kids.

Exploring the world through local field trips has long been a traditional practice in schools. Often, this grade-level adventure is seen as a highlight of the school year. Children are thrilled to spend time with peers and teachers as they discover what parts of their world look like. As teachers we had always tried to extend this aspect of field trips by making efforts to conduct weather reports from new and different locations if we were not in the classroom. (For example, snow day weather reports might come from students at home in New Jersey, or a walking trip to the library would be shared through the weather report from a student in California.) However, just as we saw the great potential to report the weather from anywhere, we knew we could build a special experience together through an upcoming field trip to the pumpkin patch in New Jersey.

Week 1: Developing Student Connection and a Kmail Invitation
The fall season presented an abundance of opportunities to explore seasonal changes as they exist in different places around the country. While both classes recognized pumpkins as traditional fall symbols, perspective of location, climate, and weather all impacted the ways in which children saw these seasonal elements. We began by creating common ground through Morning Messages and Extended Reading lessons that would drive instruction while focusing on the life cycle of a pumpkin.

During this time, Jessica was excited to announce an upcoming field trip to a local farm where the children would have time to explore a variety of activities, including picking pumpkins directly off the vines in the pumpkin patch. The children were thrilled with their upcoming experience and, unsurprisingly, asked if their California buddies (who they knew were also learning about pumpkins) would be going to pick pumpkins too. Jessica explained that the school in California was located farther away from farms where pumpkins might be growing, but she suggested that perhaps her class could do something special to include their California friends in the experience. The children eagerly agreed to compose a Kmail message to share their exciting news and ask if their buddies would like them to collect any information about their journey.

CONNECT

Guiding Questions:
- What is the connecting piece, the tie, that is bringing you together?
- What concepts or ideas help kids bridge previous learning/experiences to the next set of concepts and ideas?

Previous Discoveries and Connections:
- During a week in October, both of our classes were reading *Pumpkin, Pumpkin* by Jeanne Titherington.
- Jessica's class was going to the pumpkin patch at the farm, and it presented an opportunity for her class to reach out to Christine's class to ask what they wondered about pumpkins.

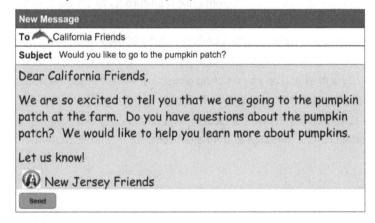

Learning Objectives: What goals do the classes share that need to be worked on?

Common Core State Standards—English Language Arts

Reading: Foundational Skills

- Read emergent-reader texts with purpose and understanding. (RF.K.4)

Writing

- With guidance and support from adults, explore a variety of digital tools to produce and publish writing, including in collaboration with peers. (W.K.6)
- With guidance and support from adults, recall information from experiences or gather information from provided sources to answer a question. (W.K.8)

Speaking and Listening

- Add drawings or other visual displays to descriptions as desired to provide additional detail. (SL.K.5)

Language

- Understand and use question words (interrogatives) (e.g., who, what, where, when, why, how). (L.K.1.D)
- Produce and expand complete sentences in shared language activities. (L.K.1.F)
- Identify real-life connections between words and their use (e.g., note places at school that are colorful). (L.K.5.C)

Technology

ISTE Standards for Students

- Global Collaborator - 7a Students use digital tools to connect with learners from a variety of backgrounds and cultures, engaging with them in ways that broaden mutual understanding and learning.
- Creative Communicator - 6c Students communicate complex ideas clearly and effectively by creating or using a variety of digital objects such as visualizations, models, or simulations.
- Creative Communicator - 6d Students publish or present content that customizes the message and medium for their intended audiences.

Exemplary Uses of Technology and Interactive Media for Early Learning (Pennsylvania Digital Media Literacy Project)
- The use of interactive media and technology tools is intentional.
- The physical environment is configured to accommodate the specific technology tool.
- Technology and interactive media offer opportunities for joint engagement, collaboration, information sharing, and conversation with peers, educators, parents, or other caregivers.
- Interactive media and technology tools are connected to the non-digital world.
- Technology tools and interactive media are used to strengthen home–school connections.
- All children, including dual language learners, children with special needs, and others, have opportunities to use and learn from available technologies.

Developmentally Appropriate Practices (NAEYC)
- Effective uses of technology and media are active, hands-on, engaging, and empowering; give the child control; provide adaptive scaffolds to ease the accomplishment of tasks; and are used as one of many options to support children's learning.
- Interactions with technology and media should be playful and support creativity, exploration, pretend play, and active play.
- Technology and media can enhance early childhood practice when integrated into the environment, curriculum, and daily routines.

Weeks 2-3: Preparing and Sharing Wonders

Christine was ready to capture the ideas and questions of children in her class as she prepared special thought-bubble papers for them to record their ideas in words and pictures. Once they had their ideas ready, they worked in groups of two or three children to communicate a focus question to their New Jersey friends via a special field trip Flipgrid. (The New Jersey students would later use this same Flipgrid space to record discoveries from the farm.) A Kmail reply message was sent to the New Jersey friends to let them know that California students had questions to share.

— WONDER —

Guiding Questions:
- How will you create wonder?
- How are you going to capture the kids' questions?

Resources and Ideas:

A Space for Wonder
- Christine's class brainstormed some questions in groups of two and three.
- Children drew exactly what those questions looked like inside their heads.
- A Flipgrid was set up to serve as another way to communicate so that the groups of California kids would be able to share their questions, and the New Jersey kids would later be able to respond with their discoveries.
- (This process offered points of focus for the children in New Jersey as they prepared to visit the farm.)

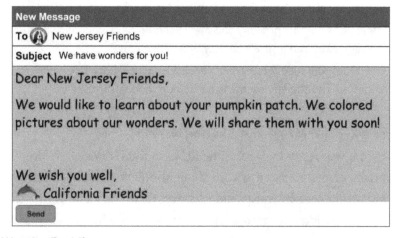

California

What else do you see at the pumpkin patch (besides pumpkins)?

New Message

To 🧑 New Jersey Friends

Subject We have wonders for you!

Dear New Jersey Friends,

We would like to learn about your pumpkin patch. We colored pictures about our wonders. We will share them with you soon!

We wish you well,
🔺 California Friends

`Send`

Wonder Buddies
- Each child in New Jersey was assigned a Wonder Buddy in their class.
- Wonder Buddies wore matching pumpkin necklaces that were numbered and had the wonder/question written.
- When children arrived at school, the Flipgrid was projected for them to see, and their Wonder Buddy Necklaces were waiting for them. Children

found their names and were able to talk with their buddies about ways in which they would try to capture their discoveries.

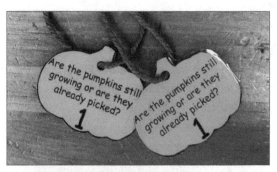

Week 4: Exploring with Wonder Buddies

To organize the actual field trip day and ensure that all questions were answered, Jessica assigned "Wonder Buddies" specific questions. The questions shared in the Flipgrid were printed out and placed on pumpkin necklaces (which also served as name tags) that the children would wear at the farm. As they toured the farm, the Wonder Buddies listened carefully and observed closely to find an answer to their question. Once a student made a discovery, Jessica used a classroom iPad to record a video of them sharing it. (These videos would later be transferred to Flipgrid for sharing with the California class.) She then placed a sticker on the student's name tag to keep track of which students had answered their questions and recorded videos.

PLAY

Guiding Question:

- How and where will the experience(s) be facilitated?

Children's Investigations at the Farm

- Instead of recording right into the field trip Flipgrid at the farm, children's discoveries were captured as short videos using the iPad and were later uploaded onto Flipgrid.

- As children shared their discovery, a sticker was placed on their necklace to show that their video had been completed, and their name was also crossed off a checklist to make sure all discoveries had been captured.

Weeks 4-5: Sharing Discoveries

Once back in the classroom, Jessica was able to organize the videos as responses in the Flipgrid space. This served as a wonderful reflection for all of the children who had been on the trip, and as a source of information for the buddy class who had anxiously been awaiting answers to their questions. Again, Kmail was used to communicate that the Flipgrid was ready for sharing. To extend the experience further, Christine printed out photos that matched the discoveries, and the children created a hands-on thinking map to organize their newly collected information.

—————————————— DISCOVER ——————————————

Guiding Question:
- What tools will you use for documentation and reflection, and how will you use them?

Ideas:
- Discoveries from the New Jersey children were matched to the California children's wonders on the grid.
- A Kmail message was composed by the New Jersey class to notify their California friends that discoveries were waiting for them.
- In order to view the flow of wonders and discoveries with ease, we created a MixTape on Flipgrid, which was shared in a New Jersey Kmail response.
- After watching the MixTape in California, children broke down all the information during a class discussion and created a thinking map.
- Children from both classes added a pumpkin bead to their Memory Strings as they reflected on the discoveries and learning that took place during this experience.

Teacher Discoveries
- Kmail creates a motivating, engaging, and safe form of digital communication for young learners to experience between classes.
- Field trips are no longer limited to one class experience in a specific location. Children can create meaningful experiences with and for other children.
- There is a natural flow between digital tools and real-world experiences that can be embraced as part of the learning process for children.

- Allowing children time and space to connect, wonder, play, and discover together empowers young learners to see how they can play the role of teacher for each other.

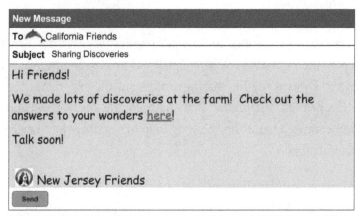

New Message

To 🐬 California Friends

Subject Sharing Discoveries

Hi Friends!

We made lots of discoveries at the farm! Check out the answers to your wonders <u>here</u>!

Talk soon!

🅐 New Jersey Friends

Send

Innovating Play Bonus Resources:
Find more at innovatingplay.world/projectplan

In each of the sections of this chapter, we have outlined experiences that have applied the Innovating Play Cycle across content areas. We have shown you some ways to play, and we hope that they inspire you to embrace this mindset as you consider possibilities for your own classroom.

Extended Learning Experience with Families

Student engagement with the weather reporting ritual soared as children surprised us and began to take the initiative to do their own weather reports on family vacations. Suddenly children were seeing what the weather was like in New York, Las Vegas, Arizona, Florida, and even Jamaica (where Jessica's student teacher recorded a weather report for the children). Families easily participated in the Flipgrid by taking videos on their phones and uploading them to the messaging space in Seesaw.

Innovating Play Bonus Resources:
Find more at innovatingplay.world/impact

As spontaneous weather reports came in, Jessica and Christine downloaded them from Seesaw and uploaded them into Flipgrid for sharing. Children had been exposed to tools and become comfortable working with them, which allowed the kids to naturally capture and share their learning in the world. Without being assigned tasks, they created the opportunity to share and connect.

Reporting the Weather While on Vacation

| Jamaica | Florida | Florida |
| Arizona | Hawaii | New York | Russia |

Learning with the #InnovatingPlay Community

Share one of your favorite science activities or projects. What connections and discoveries do students make in the process?

innovatingplay.world/bookq5

Mathematics

As rituals and routines are often established early and continue through the duration of the school year, teachers across grade levels and content areas use ongoing routines as spaces to build knowledge and scaffold learning. In early childhood and primary school classrooms, concepts such as counting the number of days of school provide the opportunity to collect, articulate, organize, and analyze data about the immediate surrounding world. These traditional practices support development in mathematical thinking while offering children the opportunity to participate in hands-on experiences to learn necessary skills and strategies.

As we mentioned earlier, when we consider the idea of innovating these types of routines, we do not advocate getting rid of the time-tested materials associated with these practices. The experiences of bundling straws or craft sticks, interacting with charts, and manipulating tactile pieces allow children to engage in creating concrete number representations. Instead of replacing content area routines, we encourage you to consider the possibilities for *enhancing* and *transforming* them.

As we consider integrating technology in the area of mathematics, we first acknowledge that we never compromise or substitute the hands-on experiences necessary for the foundation of mathematical development. You will see in this chapter that we incorporate technology into our experiences alongside concrete application of ideas. Digital tools, as they apply to mathematics as part of a collaborative classroom experience, can offer new ways to visualize and compare data that is shared between classes. In this chapter we will illustrate how reimagining simple math routines by including a collaborating class in a different location can provide opportunities to analyze, compare, and communicate mathematical ideas that are relevant and meaningful to children.

Days of School Counting

As teachers we recognize that the traditional practice of counting days of school plays an important role for young children as they develop mathematical thinking. The understanding that each successive number is one larger, the ability to compose and decompose numbers into tens and ones, and the ability to create concrete representations for place value are all inherent skills attached to recognizing the number of days children have been in school.

Innovating Play Bonus Resources: Find more at
innovatingplay.world/daysofschool
innovatingplay.world/duodaysofschool

We both continue to use traditional ways to represent and visualize this information in our classrooms. Hands-on materials and math manipulatives continue to play a role in our daily routines. Along with this, we also see the need to consider the other ways in which children take in number representations in the larger world. There are, of course, an abundance of opportunities for counting and organizing concrete objects in everyday life; however, children are also exposed to number representations in other forms, including a variety of digital spaces. If we are going to develop thinkers that can apply their understanding outside the classroom, we have a responsibility to expand the types of representations we use with our students.

Days of School Charts

In Our Classrooms

The Days of School Representation spreadsheet template was inspired by the traditional school day counting charts that contain the numeral place value breakdown of hundreds, tens, and ones. First, we complete the chart that is in the physical space in the classroom by changing the digits and adding a stick or straw to the collection. Then we transfer this information into our shared Google Sheet. Instead of doing away with the chart in the classroom, we include it because we see the value of physically manipulating the digits and the counting rods. There is also value in bringing the digit-changing piece into a spreadsheet space so children can learn how to manipulate the cells of a spreadsheet. Kids do not need to wait until they are taking an economics class in high school to be exposed to spreadsheets! This daily whole-group approach to using a spreadsheet is safe for both teachers and students because of the consistency in the way that it is used. We have customized the Days of School Representation template to reflect the details of each of our schools. Including school colors and mascot images supports even the most emergent readers in understanding how the information is organized. From the very first day of school, children in New Jersey know to look for their dog mascot in order to change the digit on their side, while children in California know to look for the Holly Avenue dolphin.

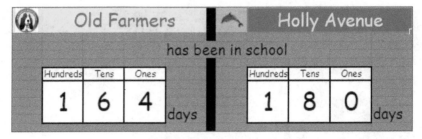

After we indicate how many days of school we have attended in their numeral form, we head into the "ten frames" sheet to add color to a cell in a ten frame to visually represent another day of school. The second sheet is conditionally formatted according to the key. Type the digit of the color you would like into the cell, and the cell will turn that color. The idea is to use a maximum of two colors per ten frame so that when the ten frame is complete you can type the addends of the ten pair into the rectangular cell located next to the ten frame.

Developing number sense, building flexibility with adding numbers to ten, and using ten frames are foundational math concepts for students. Through this ritual, children have the daily opportunity to connect and compare numbers that are meaningful to them.

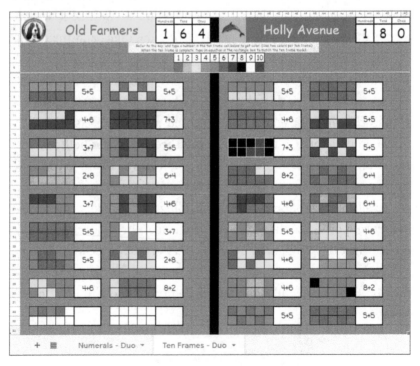

As we blend the physical and digital representations of numbers, new experiences naturally arise. Just as the Morning Message provided a space for students to learn how to work in Google Slides, the Days of School Representation provides a space for children to develop comfort and understanding of the tools within Google Sheets. Children find confidence and independence as they participate in the manipulation of the digital space.

At the highest level of the SAMR model, the Days of School Representation is redefined because it is a shared space between classrooms rather than a traditional experience that is limited to one classroom. It is in this redefined experience that we blend the physical representations, digital representations, and shared analysis of multiple sets of data. It is important to note that a collaboration between classes can exist in various forms and does not always mean that we are working in a digital space at the same time. For classes that collaborate beyond their own time zone, trying to work simultaneously could present myriad challenges. This is why we choose a balance of collaborative experiences between our classes where contributions and connections are ongoing in ways that work in both of our classrooms. Each class experiences this part of our collaboration in its own space and time, which helps children to develop a critical understanding of how to work in a collaborative group space. Digital citizenship discussions naturally occur as we reflect on appropriate ways to use the space. For example, if one class has not had the chance to complete part of the math routine because of a change in their daily schedule, we discuss as a class why it would be unfair for one class to change the space that belongs to the other class without asking. We give our interactions in digital spaces the same respect that we show interactions in physical spaces. This plants a very important foundational concept that will be critical for students, as they will be exposed to a myriad of digital creation and interaction platforms throughout their lives. Natural lessons in digital citizenship continuously present themselves as children learn to respect the space that belongs to each class, while participating in collaborative analysis.

In the Days of School Representation, children are asked to look at the concrete number representation in the classroom in conjunction with visual and symbolic representations of numbers in digital spaces. Children are able to grasp concepts quickly because the numbers have personal meaning and context, and they have participated in collecting the data. Looking at the information alone, the children might simply be restating data such as "We have been at school 164 days." As we look at data represented through collaboration, the conversation shifts to: "What is the difference between 164 and 180? How do you know? Why is that information important to you? What does it tell us about the experiences of children in different places?"

Using the prompts in the Facilitation Questions for Days of School Representation table, take time to consider the ways in which shifting your math routine supports new ways of thinking and questioning in your classroom.

Facilitation Questions for Days of School Representation

TRADITIONAL COUNTING

- How many days have we been at school?
- If we had ___ straws/sticks yesterday, how many will we have today?

ENHANCED IN GOOGLE SHEETS

Place Value Numeral Boxes:
- Which box do we click on to change the digit?
- Where is today's digit on the keyboard?
- Is it to the right or left of yesterday's number?
- Do we need to change any other boxes?
- What is the total number representing the days of school today?

Ten Frames:
- How do we change the color to represent the information?
- Which number matches the color?
- How can we represent the number sentence using the keyboard? (e.g., using the shift key to get the plus sign)
- If we had ___ in our ten frame yesterday, how many will we have today?

TRANSFORMED BY COLLABORATING WITH ANOTHER CLASS

- How many days have our friends been at school?
- Who has been at school longer?
- What is the difference between the two?
- What strategy did you use to figure it out?
- How many did our friends have yesterday? How many will they have today?
- How can we use the ten frames as evidence that they have more/fewer days than us?

When we consider shifts that support meaningful tech integration, we look carefully at the questioning and conversations that surround different types of experiences. This can provide perspective on the depth of understanding children may achieve during this time. As we move from independent math routines to offering new ways of visualizing through tech and finally consider transforming the experience by bringing our classes together, we can clearly note the shift in dialogue that is encompassed in the process of learning. As you prepare to look closely at your daily experience in mathematics with your students, here are some points to consider:

- Identify the elements of your physical classroom routines that hold the most value for you as an educator.
- Determine your comfort level in shifting your routines. Even if Google Sheets is a new space for you, treat it as a space where you can learn with your students.
- Use the template and set up a space to play. Recognize that it's OK to add to your existing routine at any point in the year.
- If you are starting later in the year, decide if you want to spend time with your students filling in information, or if you will fill it in ahead of time for children to break down and then participate in moving forward.
- Start thinking about buddy class options (see the end of Chapter 10 for finding a collaborating teacher).

Number Stories

Development of mathematical thinking in young children happens in three important stages: concrete, pictorial, and abstract. In order to develop a firm foundation in mathematics, children must have the opportunity to manipulate objects, show their thinking in pictures, and represent their ideas in mathematical symbols. As we created an interdisciplinary experience through our number stories study (which we describe next), careful thought and consideration were given to how we could capture children's natural, playful experiences to support this process. Throughout this four-week study, we embraced the opportunity to incorporate language arts goals alongside math goals with reading, writing, speaking and listening, viewing and extracting information, and devising visual representations to create and solve number stories in all three stages of development.

As we support children in becoming deep mathematical thinkers, we consider the practice of mathematics alongside the content. For young children, developing the practice of mathematics means giving them the tools they need to communicate their ideas through language. Mathematically proficient students do not just apply strategies to solve problems, they continuously make connections and ask themselves, "Does this make sense?"

Innovating Play Bonus Resources: Find more at innovatingplay.world/numberstoryboards innovatingplay.world/numberstoriesbook

Week 1: Developing Foundational Skills

During Connected Play (Chapter 7), we immerse the children in opportunities to explore number stories from a variety of perspectives. We offer experiences that help children to see the different parts and elements of number stories. Art, hands-on manipulatives, digital experiences, and games allow children to see how the components of number stories can be broken down. To expand this further, we use our playing with words centers to help children see connections between oral language, written words, and sentence structure and to provide models for mathematical thinking in the area of reading. During this time, children develop foundational skills in print concepts, phonemic awareness, and phonics and word recognition alongside the ability to process, articulate, and connect mathematical ideas.

--- CONNECT ---

Guiding Questions:

- What is the connecting piece, the tie, that is bringing you together?
- What concepts or ideas help kids bridge previous learning/experiences to the next set of concepts and ideas?
- Connecting on a Shared Learning Need: The concept of number stories is complex, and we recognize the need for it to be broken down more explicitly, with language and mathematical components, for both of our classes.

Connected Play

HOW DO NUMBER STORIES WORK?
WHAT ARE THE PARTS OF A NUMBER STORY?

Play with Technology and Communication

Felt Board Number Stories
Children use the Felt Board app to create a number story problem. They upload it to Seesaw to record the number story.

Play with Art and Expression

Number Story Setting
Children draw a setting on construction paper that will be used for a number story problem with their block people.

Play with Building and Engineering

Block People Subtraction
Children listen and solve subtraction number story problems created by Miss Pinto with the block friends.

Play with Letters and Words

Eagle-Eye Reading
Children practice the Eagle-Eye Reading Strategy by looking closely at the pictures and thinking of the first letter/sound that goes with the word for the picture.

Playing with Words

HOW DO READERS AND WRITERS USE NUMBERS AND COUNTING?

Roll and Record
Children play roll and record to practice sight words frequently found in number stories. Exposure to words builds confidence for application in mathematics.

Counting Letters
Using cards with words found in number stories, children count the number of letters. They sort, graph, and record the words according to the number of letters.

many	How
all	together?
are	there

Sentence Building
Children cut apart and rebuild the sentence. They then illustrate and label a picture to match the number and a chosen object.

How many are there now?

Number Story Guided Reading
Using little books from Reading A-Z, children work in small groups to explore number stories at differentiated reading levels.

puppy

Syllable Smash
Children use picture cards, Play-Doh, and syllable smash cards. They say the word, count the syllables, and smash the Play-Doh balls to match. Numbers are then recorded.

Learning Objectives: What goals do the classes share that need to be worked on?

Common Core State Standards—Mathematics

Operations and Algebraic Thinking

- Represent addition and subtraction with objects, fingers, mental images, drawings, sounds (e.g., claps), acting out situations, verbal explanations, expressions, or equations. (K.OA.A.1)

- Solve addition and subtraction word problems, and add and subtract within 10, e.g., by using objects or drawings to represent the problem. (K.OA.A.2)

Common Core State Standards—English Language Arts

Reading: Foundational Skills

- Follow words from left to right, top to bottom, and page by page. (RF.K.1.A)

- Understand that words are separated by spaces in print. (RF.K.1.C)

- Recognize that spoken words are represented in written language by specific sequences of letters. (RF.K.1.B)

- Count, pronounce, blend, and segment syllables in spoken words. (RF.K.2.B)

- Read common high-frequency words by sight (e.g., the, of, to, you, she, my, is, are, do, does). (RF.K.3.C)

- Read emergent-reader texts with purpose and understanding. (RF.K.4)

Writing

- Use a combination of drawing, dictating, and writing to narrate a single event or several loosely linked events, tell about the events in the order in which they occurred, and provide a reaction to what happened. (W.K.3)

Reading: Literature

- With prompting and support, identify characters, settings, and major events in a story. (RL.K.3)

Speaking and Listening

- Add drawings or other visual displays to descriptions as desired to provide additional detail. (SL.K.5)

Technology

ISTE Standards for Students

- Global Collaborator - 7a Students use digital tools to connect with learners from a variety of backgrounds and cultures, engaging with them in ways that broaden mutual understanding and learning.
- Creative Communicator - 6c Students communicate complex ideas clearly and effectively by creating or using a variety of digital objects such as visualizations, models, or simulations.
- Creative Communicator - 6d Students publish or present content that customizes the message and medium for their intended audiences.

Exemplary Uses of Technology and Interactive Media for Early Learning (Pennsylvania Digital Media Literacy Project)

- The use of interactive media and technology tools is intentional.
- The physical environment is configured to accommodate the specific technology tool.
- Technology and interactive media offer opportunities for joint engagement, collaboration, information sharing, and conversation with peers, educators, parents, or other caregivers.
- Interactive media and technology tools are connected to the non-digital world.
- Technology tools and interactive media are used to strengthen home–school connections.
- All children, including dual language learners, children with special needs, and others, have opportunities to use and learn from available technologies.

Developmentally Appropriate Practices (NAEYC)

- Effective uses of technology and media are active, hands-on, engaging, and empowering; give the child control; provide adaptive scaffolds to ease the accomplishment of tasks; and are used as one of many options to support children's learning.
- Interactions with technology and media should be playful and support creativity, exploration, pretend play, and active play.
- Technology and media can enhance early childhood practice when integrated into the environment, curriculum, and daily routines.

Weeks 2–3: Application through Creating Number Stories

After taking the time to develop connections and work with the language of number stories, we can explore possibilities for creating number stories to apply and share our math thinking. This presents the opportunity to incorporate all three stages of mathematical development into the children's work. The creation of individual number story books integrates beautifully with the process of writing development as children show their thinking in pictures, words, and sentences. At the root of this experience is the opportunity to immerse children in the concept of how sentences and equations are both symbolic representations of their thinking. Rather than isolating the developmental processes of reading, writing, and mathematical thinking, we weave them together in order to support children in developing the richest possible foundation in all areas.

Guiding Questions:

- How will you create wonder?
- How are you going to capture the kids' questions?

Idea:

Number Story Books

- Individual number story books allow children to express and explore their own curiosity as they select characters, settings, and events within their number stories. Children complete one page per day in their number story book.

As a culminating experience, a number story Flipgrid can be created between classes. The kids' videos in Flipgrid are used to assess student understanding and provide children an opportunity to publish, communicate, and support learning through collaboration. Each child has the opportunity to read and act out his or her story. Recording takes place one-on-one between each student and the teacher, allowing the teacher to provide individualized guidance and check for understanding.

--------------------------------- PLAY ---------------------------------

Guiding Question:
- How and where will the experience(s) be facilitated?

Activity
- Making Number Stories with Block People on Flipgrid

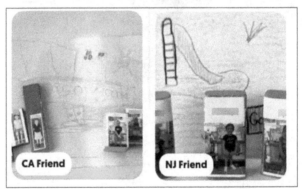

CA Friend   NJ Friend

Week 4: Listening and Solving Each Other's Number Stories

After all the number stories are recorded, children use the number story Flipgrid on the Chromebooks, along with paper-and-pencil recording sheets, to solve number stories created by their peers. At the end of this activity, children are invited to add their number story bead to their growing memory strings.

When we begin with play, we follow the natural instincts of the child. Using guidance from research on child development we focus on building thoughtful, rich, interdisciplinary experiences. This approach supports a strong foundational knowledge, practical application, and real-life learning transfer for young children. In this process we develop connected, joyful, life-long thinkers and learners with the capacity for depth in understanding, questioning, and problem-solving as it relates to their surrounding world.

DISCOVER

Guiding Question:
- What tools will you use for documentation and reflection, and how will you use them?
- Solving Each Other's Number Stories: Children view their friends' number stories, use a number path to model their thinking, and write an equation to solve.
- Memory String Bead: Children place a wooden bead with the Flipgrid symbol and personalized number sentence on their memory string necklace to remember this collaborative experience.

Extended Learning Experience with Families

As with all of our experiences, we consider families an important part of our collaboration; they are critical in keeping the Innovating Play Cycle moving forward by solidifying discoveries at home and creating new levels of connection. Another way that we bring learning experiences to families is through a shared Google Site that highlights learning that has taken place between our classrooms. (This will be discussed in more detail in Chapter 9.) After completing the number stories project over the course of several weeks, we wanted to offer families a complete look at the experience from beginning to end. We created a page on our Google Site dedicated to articulating the process of learning through-out the project. Within this documentation, we also wanted to help families understand the process of mathematical thinking and devel-opment. Rather than simply sharing what was unfolding, we offered a clear picture of why learning was approached and supported in specific ways. Creating common ground between classroom experiences and home experiences elevates the process for families as they have a deeper understanding of their child's learning as a whole.

Learning with the #InnovatingPlay Community

Share one of your favorite math activities or projects. What connections and discoveries do students make in the process?

innovatingplay.world/bookq6

Children form deep connections to their learning through multiple experiences we build. How can we prevent isolated lessons and instead put energy into creating connected experiences for kids? Share your example or idea!

innovatingplay.world/bookq7

All collaborations begin with a sense of wonder. What tools or strategies can we offer students so that they have the opportunity to wonder in meaningful and authentic ways?

innovatingplay.world/bookq8

Collaboration requires careful articulation of ideas before, during, and after the process. What are some ideas, topics, and concepts that we can offer students so that assignments can become collaborative activities or projects?

innovatingplay.world/bookq9

What are some authentic reflection strategies that can be used to support deeper learning? How does collaboration support authentic reflection?

innovatingplay.world/bookq10

Part Three

Innovating Play Unchained

*A*ll teachers have ways of inviting students into the learning space of the classroom. In early childhood and primary grades, students often unpack for the day and then engage in simple activities that allow for independence. During this time, teachers are completing a variety of housekeeping tasks such as tending to individual needs of children, taking attendance and the lunch count, and organizing logistics. Many teachers refer to this time as "morning work," as students complete simple tasks in a whole-group setting. As educators we know that every moment of the day matters. We are always looking for more time to cover content and reach standards. In this section we invite you to consider the ways in which a Connected Play time can support curriculum learning while allowing children to develop social-emotional skills and strategies through joyful and motivating experiences.

As we began to explore possibilities together, our kids' play became deeper and richer because of what they learned from each other through their shared digital space in Seesaw. Children are designing their own play experiences with the intention of sharing beyond the walls of the classroom. Their play has a new sense of purpose. Not only do they play for enjoyment, they also play with the understanding that their ideas matter because they will be communicated to an authentic audience of peers.

Jessica's students may not have been inspired to create puppets if they hadn't seen what Christine's kids were doing. Christine's kids may not have seen the depth of the value of their play had they not seen the way it transferred to others beyond their space. Children have shared ideas that have inspired play experiences in both classes. Children are taking play to the next level by discovering new ways to play and considering the ideas of children in the other class. This allows them to develop not only a rich knowledge base, but a rich understanding of the diversity of thinking in the world.

As teachers this is an area that we are just starting to explore together. Within these possibilities, we have the potential to change the way children play and connect on a global scale. If children learn to play together from different locations, then there is the potential for them to bring this idea of working in different places as grown-ups when they are in the workforce. Children who learn to play together globally may be the ones who are more likely to work together in virtual spaces with new levels of compassion, understanding, and connection. This is why we start from the beginning. The foundation we help to shape and create in our youngest learners has the potential to significantly impact the world we live in and the physical and digital worlds we continue to create together.

Connected Play

onnected Play gives kids the opportunity to activate prior knowledge and make connections through art, exploration, creation, manipulation, experimentation, observation, language, technology, and communication. Within the first twenty minutes of the day, we focus on helping children make these connections by offering them a variety of ways to process and create while they work individually and interact with peers.

As you think about planning and preparing for Connected Play, there are some bigger-picture questions to keep in mind:

- How can open-ended materials support creativity in communication and reflection?
- How can observations of children's natural learning patterns guide instruction throughout the day?
- How can play-based experiences support connections between social, academic, and emotional growth?
- How can technology be woven into play meaningfully?

As teachers we all have different strategies for planning and developing experiences for our students. Since Connected Play is an opportunity to integrate content areas and address the specific needs of a class of learners, the first thing to do is check in with the needs of students. We like to consider three different ways to build connections through content, although keep in mind that there are no limits to the ways you can foster connections for students.

Building Connections Through Content

THEMATIC

Perhaps there is an area of focus that students will benefit from having time to ponder as you prepare to start the day. A concentrated area of thematic study or an upcoming experience, such as an event or field trip, that the children will be having together provides the perfect foundation for Connected Play.

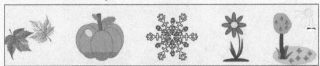

LITERATURE-BASED

Literacy experiences such as shared texts, poems, songs, and nursery rhymes all provide great starting points for Connected Play. Whether it's an authentic text or part of a district literacy program, a specific text can be a point of connection from which you can build.

LEARNING STANDARDS

Consider standards in any of the curricular areas in which your students need more instructional or processing time. This is an opportunity to gain time for diving deeper into any of these areas.

Once you have your point of connection, you can begin to develop ideas for experiences you would like to offer. We often planned the hands-on pieces first and then considered how to integrate technology to enhance the experience and make further connections.

Innovating Play Bonus Resources: Find more at innovatingplay.world/connectedplayboards

The key to developing rich technology experiences through connection is often just having all of the other building blocks—like hands-on experiences—in place first. The term "blended learning" is often used solely in association with technology integration. While we will have a strong focus on strategies for integrating meaningful technology in this chapter, we will begin with the idea that blended learning means bringing together *all* kinds of experiences so that children have a variety of ways to create, process, and visualize learning.

Building Connections through Different Types of Play

There are four types of play for building connection during Connected Play: Art and Expression, Building and Engineering, Letters and Words, and Technology and Communication. We value these types of play and wanted to ensure that we offered children opportunities within each category on a frequent basis. On occasion, we would switch out a type of play and include another type. There are no limits to the ways you can play! Think about the types of play you value and what you want to provide your students in your version of Connected Play.

As we give more detail about the types of play and their value, you will also find specific examples that we took directly from one of our connected experiences. At one point in the year we were learning about our community in relation to the space in which we live—city or country—and literally tapping into our senses to figure out how we take in the world. It was a bonus for us to embrace this focus area together, because Christine's class is located in the city, and Jessica's class is located in the country. The featured text was from the Fountas and Pinnell Shared Reading Big Book series, titled *City Kid, Country Kid.* (A similar text with the same title, that is more accessible, is written by Julie Cummins.)

To solidify the connection and focus instruction, we also include essential questions that help students retain what they learn whenever possible. The question that was supporting student learning during this particular week was: "How can I learn more about the world?"

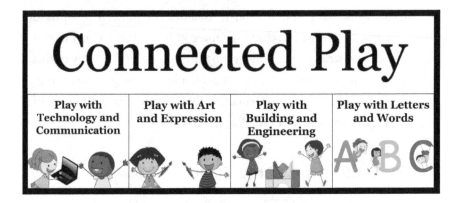

Connected Play

Play with Technology and Communication	Play with Art and Expression	Play with Building and Engineering	Play with Letters and Words

Play with Art and Expression

As we expose children to diverse learning opportunities, we ensure that there are ample possibilities for hands-on creation and discovery. Here we consider ways that children can retell, represent, extend, experience, and process the connection between the activity and the learning focus. There are many wonderful resources available for art experiences that support connection. Whether they involve exposing children to textures, techniques, materials, or open-ended or specific processes, art and expression create space to both protect an artistic mindset and uncover opportunities for learning. We have found that many art experiences can be effectively used to reach ELA standards.

Sandpaper Art

Children explore drawing with crayons on sandpaper. Learners consider the way texture affects interactions between materials and develop descriptive vocabulary.

Essential Question:

- What if all objects and materials felt and interacted in the same way?

"I Can" Statement:

- I can use my sense of touch to discover more about my world.

Skills Practiced:

- Asking questions, making observations, and gathering information to support thinking about experiences and problems.

- Exploring a variety of sensory materials, processes, and application methods that provide opportunities for discovering solutions to creative and real-world problems.

- Identifying real-life connections to words and their use as they apply to hands-on experiences.

Play with Building and Engineering

The experience of learning with building and engineering is often linked to math and science. Creating a consistent space to explore STEM (Science, Technology, Engineering, and Math) activities means that they are not treated as separate experiences, but rather as meaningful extensions that are woven into learning. The more we can support children in seeing connections between learning experiences, the more we can help their learning to stick and guide them in developing richer schemata about the world.

Pan Flute Songs

Children use pan flutes made with straws to explore sound and compose songs using color and number patterns.

Essential Question:

- How do sounds in our world provide information about people, places, and experiences?

"I Can" Statement:

- I can listen to discover more about my world.

Skills Practiced:

- Predicting, planning, and observing changes in sound.
- Activating prior knowledge and making connections between sound and personal experiences.
- Developing listening skills.

Play with Letters and Words

Teachers are always looking for more time to support growth for readers in the classroom. Whether developing specific skills and strategies for younger children or comprehension experiences for more advanced readers, a strong literacy focus is essential at all levels and even across many content areas. Instead of creating separate literacy experiences, we offer Connected Play as the space where we can help children see context for reading.

I Spy…

Children use manipulatives along with Seesaw photo, caption, and recording tools to create I Spy pictures to share with families and buddies.

Essential Question:

- Why are words and detailed visual descriptions important in understanding and communicating about our world?

"I Can" Statement:

- I can use what I see to create, share, and discover more about my world.

Skills Practiced:

- Spelling simple words phonetically and drawing on knowledge of sound–letter relationships.
- Adding drawings or other visual displays to descriptions, as desired, to provide additional detail.
- Communicating ideas using oral language.
- Asking and answering questions.
- Communicating information and ideas to multiple audiences using digital media.

Play with Technology and Communication

Technology offers students another way to visualize, take in, process, extend, and create. While we would never advocate that technology take the place of any of the other Connected Play components, we absolutely value the way that technology has the potential to enhance and transform learning in ways that would have at one time been inconceivable in the classroom. Later in this chapter we will look at specific planning strategies we can employ to best use technology for connected learning.

Animal Research Drawing

Children use drawing videos to extend research projects on farm animals. Selecting an animal from this list allows children to access resources to explore and draw independently.

Essential Question:
- Why is it important to research, communicate, and share about different animals and places in the world?

"I Can" Statement:
- I can research and collect important information.

Skills Practiced:
- Participating in shared research and writing projects.
- Using technology to enhance productivity.
- Recalling information from experiences or gathering information from provided sources to answer a question.
- Adding drawings to descriptions, as desired, to provide additional detail.
- Developing a model to represent the needs of animals and the places they live (NGSS).

Connected Play experiences provide multiple ways to take in a common connection. It's our time to reach all learners through a variety of approaches that stimulate curiosity, depth, and a sense of purpose as they develop knowledge about the world. In addition, it is a way to engage learners from the moment the day begins. Not one second of learning time is wasted as students eagerly look to explore connections every day. It is through these connections that they begin to prepare themselves for the learning of the day. **Beginning the day with Connected Play means that all learners have the chance to activate prior knowledge before lessons take place.** All learners have the chance to see their learning within a context. All learners have a chance to engage in a variety of kinesthetic, tactile, visual, and auditory experiences that allow them to take in information in ways that meet individual and collective needs.

Instead of seeing Connected Play as "extra" we encourage teachers to see it as a way of reframing what they already do. Rather than seeing it as losing time for other things, we encourage you to see it as gaining time for depth. With the increasing push for academic rigor, this time provides a way for teachers to both meet those expectations and offer what we know all learners need. In providing children with this time and experience, we protect their ability to navigate learning with their hearts, bodies, and minds.

Extended Anecdote

When we shine a light on play as an important part of the educational process for young children, we establish a critical part of the culture within and between classrooms. In our classrooms children come to see that their play is valued. With this, families begin to take more careful note of the connections between their child's play at home and the experience of learning. These connections often become more apparent as families begin to use the tools we offer for sharing experiences between home and school. Having a specific communication tool (such as Seesaw) that allows families to easily open up communication on their side adds a level of safety and comfort to the bond between students, caregivers, and teachers.

Innovating Play Bonus Resources: Find more at innovatingplay.world/connectedplayvideo

Evidence of this became clear one morning when Jessica was preparing for the day of school ahead. One of the families sent a notification via Seesaw that the kindergarten student had been preparing for the upcoming day of learning by building with special blocks at home. Instead of waiting to share about it when he got to school, he asked his mother to send a photo with a voice note so that he could explain his creation. Jessica was thrilled to see that he had sought this connection on his own, had recognized the value of his process and creation with block play, and had known how to use the tool that was in place to communicate with ease. She also recognized the important way that he was getting his brain ready to start the day. In her reply, she furthered the connection for the day by attaching a JPEG of the Connected Play slide that he would see when entering the classroom. She explained that he would be building a shade structure in the Building and Engineering center that day and encouraged him to think about how the strategies he used when he was building with blocks at home could be applied when he got to school. In these simple and spontaneous communications, we see the way that the student–teacher connection through play offers purposeful and meaningful context for learning as it occurs within and beyond the classroom.

Organization and Workflow

In this section we will share our strategies for using Google Slides to organize and facilitate Connected Play experiences. In Google Slides we create a visual representation consisting of four to five activities. The slide also includes small groups of children's names in order to organize participation in activities—this is known as a play board. Throughout this book, you will find that we have created and offered ways to use technology not only to support student learning, but to improve teacher facilitation and workflow as well.

Innovating Play Bonus Resources:
Find more at innovatingplay.world/connectedplay

Our play boards are designed to organize each type of center and the groups of students for one week. In Google Slides you can insert images and include a title in order to visually communicate to emerging readers the center type they will be engaging in for the day.

Connected Play	Focus Question: How can I learn more about the world around me?		
Play with Technology and Communication	Play with Art and Expression	Play with Building and Engineering	Play with Letters and Words
• Sarah	• Ramon	• Rebecca	• John
• Ashley	• Nancy	• Patricia	• Sylvia
• Anthony	• James	• Robert	• Charles
• Margaret	• Brian	• Mary	• Zachary
• Kenneth	• Susan	• Chris	• Sandra
• Michelle	• Brandon	• George	• Laura

Since we introduce our point of connection on Monday, Connected Play centers start on Tuesday. As mentioned earlier, you can set up your play board while you plan for your week so it is ready to go on Tuesday. Once the first day's centers are completed, you can use the same board and shift the text boxes (containing student names) over a column each day for the rest of the week.

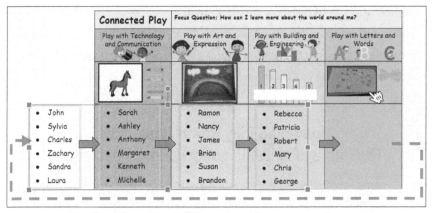

Rotation of students will vary based on your preference.
Tip: To select multiple text boxes at the same time, use the Shift key.

By tapping into the foundation created in Extended Reading, Connected Play creates rich instructional opportunities to connect learning across content areas. Adding play boards to the Morning Message slide deck can also maximize efficiency in moving between experiences. The Connected Play board serves as an introductory slide for the day.

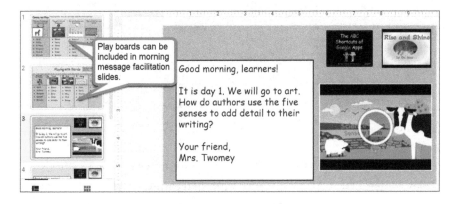

Demo Videos for Centers

In an attempt to keep center explanations concise and accessible (viewable from anywhere), we started to record video instructions via Seesaw. Oftentimes, on Tuesday mornings we recorded Connected Play centers before the kids came in. When the kids arrived, we played the demo videos. Alternatively, videos can be shared ahead of time with families to prepare children for learning.

Taking the time to do this is good for many reasons:

- While students were watching the videos, we were able to ensure students were paying attention. This decreased chances of interruptions.
- Absent students could access videos from home via Seesaw and could come back to school knowing what was expected of them with our centers.
- If we were ever absent on a Tuesday morning, Connected Play could continue, as the substitute would play our videos for the kids (we used the "Share Item" link from the post in Seesaw and included the link in the play board).

Because families had access to hear the directions, they knew what we were working on in class and why we were doing a particular activity. We used the caption feature to share more about the skills being highlighted in a given activity.

An All-Around Win

We understand how precious teacher time is and the ongoing question "Is this worth my time and energy?" that exists when creating an experience. Just like you, we also know how rewarding it feels to be in the moment with students as they happily experience what you took the time to set up for them. There are a number of "wins" in facilitating Connected Play students and teachers.

Benefits for Children

- Clear and consistent routines
- Sense of safety in learning through play-based experiences
- Activation of prior knowledge for academic concepts to be covered throughout the day
- Emergent literacy exposure through pictures and words on the play board

- Opportunity to explore and experience fine arts and visual arts during learning experiences
- Ability to self-direct
- Development of independence
- Guidance in appropriate play practices and social interaction in conjunction with academic concepts
- Time to revisit and solidify understanding of previously addressed concepts
- Time to discover and explore natural interests

Benefits for Teachers

- Play boards can be created as part of the planning process from any space at any time
- Reorganization and rotation of groups happens with ease
- Play boards can be personalized, saved, and built upon to meet the needs of learners from week to week and year to year
- Clear routines and independence create time and space for individualized and small-group instruction to meet the needs of learners
- A variety of academic skills, concepts, and strategies can be covered within this format, allowing for engaging, meaningful, and efficient learning opportunities.
- Time can be used to complete beginning-of-the-day teacher tasks while children engage in meaningful experiences
- Time can be used to document experiences to share with families and/or identify interests and connect with children
- Play boards can easily be shared between teachers to allow for collaboration in planning and facilitating experiences
- Developmentally appropriate play experiences for young children can be preserved and protected within a realistic framework

Blending Tech with Connected Learning Experiences

While many of the Connected Play experiences may be familiar and comfortable for teachers of young children, the technology piece may create the greatest source of wonder. Instead of thinking of technology as "extra," we encourage you to see it as another playground with endless options for how to play. Tech provides another way of seeing, experiencing, manipulating, visualizing, and interacting with the world. Playing with technology allows us to imagine brand-new possibilities to play. Ideas and experiences that once lived in our imaginations can now appear in front of us, building new possibilities and deeper connections as learners.

In this section we present three different ways of approaching technology experiences for Connected Play. While each level of experiences provides different ways to integrate technology, we value every one of them for what they provide learners. One experience should never be seen as "better" than another, as they all contribute to possibilities for connection in different ways.

Blending Tech with Connected Learning Experiences

TECH FOR EXPOSURE

A game or experience that could connect thematically or academically. Typically it is used for introduction and practice.

TECH THAT GROWS WITH YOU

A game or experience in which children have an account that allows them to come back and play as skills develop.

TECH THAT INVITES CREATION

Open-ended tools that offer a blank canvas for creation so learning experiences can be customized.

Tech for Exposure

We define a Tech for Exposure opportunity as a game or experience that could connect thematically or academically. Typically it is used for introduction and practice. On their own, these experiences may support skills and strategies or allow children the opportunity to develop comfort and dexterity in navigating digital spaces. They may feel "safe" for teachers in that most children will independently manipulate, problem-solve, and support each other in navigating the activity.

Guiding Questions to Expand the Experience:

- How can I connect this tool to a hands-on experience?
- How can I connect it to a thematic or literature-based study?
- How can I elevate it by using it in conjunction with other tools?

TOOL	CONNECTION AND ACTIVITY
QuiverVision 	As we explored nonfiction text through a thematic book on fruit, children had the opportunity to create still life drawings in the art center during Connected Play. Drawings focused on observing and recreating a basket of fruit provided at the table. Creations were then brought to life using the Quiver app.
ABCya.com 	During our study of snow and winter weather, children created snowman pictures using abcya.com. After creating their pictures, children took a screenshot of the image and moved it to Seesaw. Using the label tool in Seesaw, students used developmental spelling to add labels to pictures. Images were shared with the teacher and families upon approval of the completed activity.
LetterSchool 	As we explored thematic Halloween experiences, children used hands-on and digital tools for letter identification and formation. Children began by selecting a letter card and working on trays with googly eyes to practice letters. Once they formed the letter on the tray, they found the corresponding letter in the LetterSchool app to listen to the name and corresponding sound. They then practiced forming the letter by tracing it in three different levels on the screen.

Tech That Grows with You

Tech That Grows with You is a step up from Tech for Exposure in that it is a game or experience where children have an account that allows them to come back and play as skills develop. These digital spaces may be district requirements or platforms that children can access at home as well as at school. They can provide important opportunities for differentiation and self-pacing that support all students.

Guiding Questions to Expand the Experience:

- When is an appropriate time to introduce this tool so that it is meaningful to the children?
- How can the ongoing experience be woven into instruction and made available to children at home and at school?

TOOL	CONNECTION AND ACTIVITY
Raz-Kids 	During our literacy study of "Twinkle, Twinkle, Little Star" children began this center experience by listening to the read-aloud version of the level F book *Constellations in the Stars.* After hearing the book, they used constellation picture cards and pushpins to develop fine motor skills. They first used a highlighter to mark each focus star and then used pushpins to create a small hole in each space showing the star in the constellation. When completed, the paper could be held up to the light, and the constellation shape would appear.
Teach Your Monster to Read 	During our character study, children read the book *Love Monster*. In connection to this experience, they were introduced to the online reading program Teach Your Monster to Read. Children were able to design their own monster character and work their way up through leveled reading experiences designed to grow with them as readers.
Kodable 	During our exploration of December holidays, we considered ways that people show kindness and communicate from far away. As we wrote holiday postcards to our buddies across the country, we looked closely at maps to determine ways in which packages and letters are sent around the world. Kodable was introduced at this time as a way to explore coding as a map that computers follow. Connections were made to sequencing steps and developing clear directions in order to complete both physical and digital tasks.

Tech That Invites Creation

Kids get to be the producers when they engage in Tech That Invites Creation. These open-ended tools offer a blank canvas for creation so learning experiences can be customized. The digital spaces lend themselves to experiences across content areas and grade levels. They provide tools that allow students and teachers to create together in very specific ways that allow for expansion of concepts and reimagining possibilities.

Guiding Questions to Expand the Experience:

- What experiences can we create that are specific to the community of learners?
- How can children contribute to the creation?
- How can open-ended tech build deeper connections in order to support academic/social/emotional growth?
- How can we develop experiences that connect learners between classrooms?

TOOL	CONNECTION AND ACTIVITY
Google Slides 	During our fruit-themed study, children were introduced to the artwork of Giuseppe Arcimboldo. As teachers we wanted to create a specific space for students to explore and visualize using art as inspiration. We selected Google Slides and built a Fruit Face Creations template. Children first selected a fruit "head" slide. Then they used keyboard shortcuts to manipulate the size and rotation of different fruits and vegetables. This enabled them to create unique artwork reflective of different expressions and feelings while developing their expertise in Google Slides.

Google Sheets 	During our literacy study of the nursery rhyme "Mary, Mary, Quite Contrary," children worked in Google Sheets to explore the template Making Ten: Flower Edition. Children used the colored key to choose two colors of flowers that they wanted to include in their garden. They typed the corresponding numbers into the ten flowers, created an equation to match their model, and checked their answer by typing the equals sign like you would a formula.
Flipgrid 	As part of an extended study on number stories, children created, wrote, modeled, and recorded on Flipgrid to share their ideas. Children from both classes participated in creating number story videos using block people as props to tell their number story. Children then listened to each other's number stories and used paper and pencil to solve and record.

As you prepare for technology integration within Connected Play (or any other content area throughout the day), this breakdown can help you to prevent technology from becoming an isolated experience. Whether you are working with young children or students in more advanced grades, people learn best and information sticks when it is connected and woven together with context.

As educators we have the potential to support all students in experiencing technology beyond passive consumption. Through our work with even the youngest children in the classroom we have discovered the ways in which we can shape how children see technology in the classroom and beyond. They choose technology as a tool for expression, creation, and connection and associate it with song, movement, learning, and joy. They see it as a way to capture and share experiences, which helps them to see their own value in contributing to their learning and the learning of those around them. When we remove barriers and limits to learning through technology, we change the way children view themselves and the potential for what they will produce and create in the world someday.

Learning with the #InnovatingPlay Community

What are your students learning about?
Share an example of how you are building
connections and/or context!
innovatingplay.world/bookq11

Consider an area of focus for learning. What
Connected Play experiences could you build around
the focus area to enrich instruction and learning
opportunities for your students?
innovatingplay.world/bookq12

Community Play

L earning through play can happen throughout the day with any subject, for any grade level, and with a variety of learning tools. As often as we try to make our classrooms student-driven and personalize experiences to meet the needs of our kids during teacher-planned lessons, these cannot be the only kinds of experiences we offer. To reach, inspire, motivate, and drive learning forward we need to allow time for student choice in learning and play.

Choice-based play opportunities for young children can provide the missing pieces of learning for teachers and students. This is the time when we see into the hearts and minds of our learners. It is the space for them to take their learning deeper by transferring and applying what they have connected with during lessons and experiences. It is their opportunity to show us what they want to explore further, discover, and communicate. It is their chance to shift the ownership of their learning by making choices and decisions that belong to them.

Despite the importance of all this, providing time for explorative play is often seen as "extra" or the thing we can skip when everything else takes more time than we, as teachers, had planned. We would argue that time to play should not be the extra thing, it should be the main thing from which all our other instruction is driven. If we closely observe our children during play, we will learn:

- What interests them
- How they interact with others
- What they avoid
- What learning spaces work best for them
- Who they work well with
- What challenges them
- How they transfer their learning
- What they are ready to learn
- How they treat others
- How they use executive functioning skills
- How they participate within a community

We learn who children are when we listen, interact, and thoughtfully observe them at play.

Nurturing Intentional Play

Teachers have many names for dedicated playtime experiences in the classroom. From "recess" to "free play" to "choice time," the language of this dedicated time reflects our values as we communicate the experience to children. In our classrooms, we choose the title of Community Play. The term we use to describe this time is both intentional and layered. "Community Play" means we are essentially creating a model of the world from which children can safely explore and discover. They are working within the classroom community and learning what it means to participate in the larger world. This is why we have areas of the classroom that simulate different experiences that children might have in the real world.

In this space, children begin to explore as artists, engineers, writers, mathematicians, scientists, and caregivers. It is important to note that technology can be integrated into any of the play areas, just as technology can be integrated into a variety of jobs in real life. With our Community Play design, children can bring in Chromebooks or iPads to access various apps and resources as needed. This gives them the potential to either enhance their play, document their play to reflect and share with others, or revisit tools from classroom experiences during the day to further their connections to their learning.

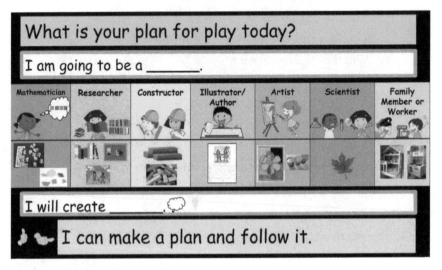

Community Play holds a special energy of independence, personality, and style that truly belongs to each unique group of students. As you prepare to read the details of the following play experiences, we invite you to first think of your own classroom. It may be a classroom you are currently in, one you may like to create moving forward, or a space you would like to support a fellow educator in developing. Consider the students who will play in this space.

Begin by selecting a few specific children whom you would like to nurture through play, and keep them in mind as you read. Visualize the ways in which they might be drawn to any of these experiences. Perhaps one of the scenarios inspires them to follow a more specific avenue to delve deeper into their creative expression. Take note of your ideas and reactions as possible points of action. Consider what you know about your students and ways you might want to scaffold their exploration. Be ready to make meaningful connections to the ways in which the possibilities here might offer new options for deeper learning and teaching through play.

A Window into Community Play in Jessica's Classroom

There is a happy buzz of movement in our kindergarten class. Chatter fills the dramatic play area as a story the children would like to perform begins to come to life. The story is about animals in a forest, and the main character is a ladybug. They spend several minutes navigating the supporting roles, along with the flow of the storyline. During their conversation, they grab an iPad and open up Book Creator to begin to record their ideas with photos and voice buttons. They turn to the children in the art area to ask, "What do we have to build a forest?" The artists begin to pull out open-ended materials and negotiate which types of materials would be best to create a forest over by their cubbies. The children in the dramatic play area use the drawing tool to sketch out their ideas in their digital book and then visit the art center. They collaborate on how to move forward.

I am on stage.

In the writing center, three children overhear the excitement about the forest story and ask if they can create tickets for the show. I ask them how they would like to do that and they brainstorm different ways they could make them. They settle on working in Google Drawing on Chromebooks. Here they can design a ticket that looks real and then duplicate it to make multiples. They beam

One Ticket
The Ladybug in the Forest

Mrs. Twomey's Classroom

2:00 Friday

with pride as they create authentic tickets for the performance. There is a spirit of cooperation, excitement, and ownership.

In the reading area, two little girls are snuggled in a rocking chair with an iPad. They are using the Draw and Tell app to draw and record a song they are writing about a trip to the movies. They jump back and forth from acting out the movie with the puppets in the library corner to recording their ideas in the app. They negotiate, perform, and reflect by listening to their

recording. They talk about what they like and problem-solve what does not meet expectations. Music and giggles fill the air.

The math center hosts three little boys. One is logged into Google Classroom on the Chromebook where he has accessed his pixel art creation in Google Sheets (template by Alice Keeler). The other little boys use Snap Cubes to create characters inspired by the one on the sheet. They are engrossed in conversation about the story that will take place with the characters they created. They make plans to place a photo of their Snap Cube creations into their

Seesaw portfolios, and they negotiate what each of them will say about it in their voice note. They consider ways to connect the completed pixel art to photos of their real-life creation.

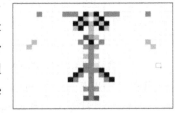

The block center houses a variety of building materials carefully constructed, balanced, and manipulated by individuals and groups of children. One little boy is carefully moving animals within the zoo he built. He stops every few moments to take photos of the animals in slightly different locations. I decide not to interrupt the process, but to back away and see what would happen. As a teacher I carefully observe and make thoughtful decisions about when to scaffold and when to move back and allow the child to work independently.

When the kids have left for the day, I log into Seesaw to approve any pending additions the children have made to their portfolios. I notice a stop-motion movie that has been uploaded by the boy in the block center. I open it up and am amazed by the creation that shows the animals in our block center magically racing across the rug. I have only introduced the Stop Motion app once. I quickly approve it with a note to the family about the independent, self-initiated process he undertook.

Later that evening, I notice a comment from the family sharing the excitement at their dinner table when the little boy shared the story with his siblings. They watched the magic of his imagination come to life as they viewed the video together. The learning transfer has happened. Play has been experienced, elevated, reflected upon, and shared in an authentic way. When we integrate purposeful play with meaningful use of technology and social scaffolding, we are Innovating Play.

Imagining New Possibilities for Play

The highest-quality play will come when children are given sufficient time, when they determine their own direction, and when they have guidance and support that scaffolds their process. This scaffolding can come from a grown-up playing intentionally side-by-side with a child, offering the appropriate level of support. In the past, this scaffolding came more often from children's natural free play experiences together outside of school: Older children would model for younger children, allowing them a chance to develop their understanding of interaction, negotiation, and social rules for play.

As schedules have become more driven by the culture of our lives, time for play outside of school is often replaced by lessons, practices, and busy schedules. Passive screen time now sometimes replaces personal interaction. Instead of blaming the circumstances or the screen, we have the opportunity as educators to recognize that the dynamics of social experiences for children are in need of redefinition. Where many may see limits, we can choose to see possibilities.

With these ideas in mind, we asked ourselves the following questions as we prepared to explore new levels of play between our classrooms:

- How can we deepen play experiences by offering children access to tools to document and extend play?
- How can we give children opportunities to scaffold play experiences for each other?
- How can we support the larger picture of digital culture and digital citizenship by starting with authentic experiences and connecting the natural instincts of the child?
- How can we involve and support families with the process of connecting through play?

In order to explore these possibilities, we knew that we needed to be ready to turn ownership over to our students. We needed to trust the foundation that we built with them through our shared daily routines and rituals and the learning experiences we used to make connections across content areas. We reflected on how we had provided authentic models for collaboration and interaction in digital spaces. It was time to allow students to create their own meaningful experiences and practice empathy and digital citizenship through their play. The children would need their own space to share so that their ideas and experiences would not only be experienced by their peers in the moment, but also by their families and their friends from across the country—beyond the classroom.

Exploring Play Together

The first action we took to connect our students through their natural play was creating a shared Seesaw class. For us, the key was providing a space where children and families were already comfortable (since we had both used Seesaw with our individual classes) from which we could build. We wanted the process to focus on the experience of play rather than on the interaction with the tool itself. As we introduced the possibilities to the children, they quickly found new inspiration both to share ideas and to begin to explore and discover in new ways. This was shown time and time again as children would thoughtfully reach out to each other for connection. Children recognized each other, lifted each other up, validated ideas and experiences, and scaffolded discovery. In the following sections, we offer a variety of examples that illustrate the types of shared play experiences we were able to guide and nurture between our classrooms and families.

Sharing During Community Play

After having learned a series of holiday songs for a school performance and enjoying the newfound discovery of making special puppets in their classroom, Christine's children recorded a musical performance with their puppets and shared it with their friends in New Jersey. When Jessica's class watched the video before playing the following day, new motivation for the art center quickly emerged. It was not long before one of the little girls in Jessica's class shared that she was ready to record her creation, because she wanted her buddy to see what he had inspired her to create. She was excited to share what she had done and also recognized the value in giving back and reciprocating in both physical and digital spaces.

When children have the ability to play between classrooms in a variety of ways, they develop a clear purpose for what they want to achieve during playtime. This new type of play opens up options for children to teach and learn from each other, along with opportunities to foster creativity and discovery. In this experience, children, teachers, and families each develop a natural sense of accountability and reciprocation as they come to view themselves as valuable contributors to the educational process. In our shared Seesaw space, students have ongoing direction and purpose for playing together. It is this dynamic that supports them in scaffolding play for each other and ultimately leads to their discovery of richer and more intentional play.

Sharing Activities Being Done in Class

While Community Play is based on student choice, children often use this time to check in on the shared Seesaw class. It is during this time that they see what their buddies have responded to or shared. This sometimes means that academic experiences that have been shared at different points in the school day resurface and lead to further exploration during Community Play. Shared experiences can also spark inspiration for additional lessons.

The ability to capture the learning process on video provides children the opportunity to solidify their understanding of concepts by modeling for others. In this math experience, children in Jessica's class worked with partners to play the "Hiding Bears Game" to practice seeing and identifying pairs of ten. As children worked together Jessica recorded video clips of interactions. Although the original intention was to share with families in Seesaw, this became a wonderful opportunity to use video clips to share the game with children in California as well.

Sharing with families and collaborating peers in another classroom adds an element of meaningful motivation to children's work. Playing the role of teacher and learner in this scenario ensures that children are both completing the activity and articulating clearly. After videos were uploaded to the shared Seesaw class, Christine was able to create the game for her students and use the video clips from the children in New Jersey to provide directions and modeling.

Sharing Special Events at School

All classrooms have opportunities to recognize and celebrate milestones for learning. When we give children a voice beyond the classroom to help recognize their process, we shape their sense of self as valuable contributors to their educational experience. As the children in California reached their hundredth day of school earlier in the school year than the students in New Jersey, videos of their project presentations were uploaded to the shared Seesaw space. While this sharing provided an authentic audience for the children in California, it also provided inspiration and the opportunity to express pride and excitement for the accomplishments of others as the children in New Jersey viewed the videos.

Sharing from Home

Inviting families to participate in the shared Seesaw space can change the dynamic of learning and conversation from outside the classroom as well. Not only do families get to see what is shared between children in the classroom, they have the opportunity to initiate sharing from home through Seesaw messaging. As our year progressed, students enjoyed sharing videos and photos from home, which

were then uploaded into the class space for sharing. In this example, a little girl from New Jersey shares her engineering project with all of her peers in New Jersey and California. She describes her process and models how her creation works as she articulates her accomplishment with clarity and excitement. Family sharing from home provides rich opportunity for conversation from a global perspective. Children listen carefully to each other for inspiration and start to recognize more fully what makes their experience unique and important. Caregivers are able to scaffold learning from home as they participate in rich conversation and appropriately model digital interaction outside the classroom.

Sharing Kid-Created Books

Feedback that is both timely and meaningful is critical for learners across content areas. Through the shared Seesaw class, children are able to share their work and receive feedback from multiple sources. In this example, students in California uploaded videos to share little books that they were creating as part of the writing process. Placing videos in the shared space meant that writers had an authentic audience for validation, feedback, and support. Teachers from both New Jersey and California were able to leave voice comments for children to support their efforts, and because their writing was also shared with buddies, students were also able to receive feedback from peers in the other class. Families were included in the process, as they had the opportunity to not only view their child's work but to also hear the levels of feedback and support offered from a variety of people experiencing the learning process together.

Keeping Buddies Connected

As part of our classroom collaboration each child is paired with a buddy from the partner class. In addition to teacher-initiated buddy experiences, children are invited to use the shared Seesaw space to connect with each other during Community Play. Along with the opportunity for students to share their own ideas and experiences, teachers have the opportunity to quietly offer students a look at the impact of their connection. Teachers can use photos to capture the process of the buddy check-in. Photographs capture facial expressions and body language, which help to deepen the connection and the students' understanding of how they impact others.

Learning with the #InnovatingPlay Community

What does choice-based play look like in your learning environment? What types of opportunities are there for students to share their play with others?

innovatingplay.world/bookq13

Sharing Play with Families

Educators facilitate and witness countless learning experiences with their students. Oftentimes we are in the moment with students as they navigate these experiences. Along the way we are capturing the process of learning that is taking place, whether through pictures, videos, student samples, or something else. When the experience is complete, those pieces deserve to be acknowledged, celebrated, and shared together!

As educators we can clearly see connections in learning, but the process as a whole may not be transparent to students and especially their families. One way to meet this need to bridge connections is to create Extended Learning Experiences. These Extended Learning Experiences can be designed to activate prior knowledge for students and families to think about before learning takes place, as a window into an ongoing project, or as a way to reflect on a culminating experience or special project. Just as we carefully design our lessons for our students, it is important to think about the students' families and how to reach them as part of our learning community.

As we prepare to look deeper into learning beyond the classroom through family sharing, we begin by acknowledging the variations, challenges, and unique qualities of family populations. Working with families is a responsibility that all educators have. As each child enters our classroom, we must remember that families form the foundation of our work. Every family that comes to us is comprised of individuals who have been a part of the education system in some way. They bring prior knowledge, expectations, and widely varying comfort levels with school. Before reading further, we invite you to consider your specific population of families. There may be considerable variation even within one classroom of students. Just as we differentiate for our students, when we extend learning to families, we are intentional about offering a range of possibilities to support learning connections between home and school.

We begin by asking ourselves:

- In what ways can we nurture children and families with feelings of comfort for the process of classroom learning?
- How can we offer possibilities for conversations and extensions that bring learning home in meaningful and practical ways?
- How can we give families a voice in their child's learning?
- How can we create a culture of learning that exists within and beyond the classroom so that all participants feel connected and valued?

As educators we have the opportunity to serve as models for this approach to family learning beyond the classroom. As with any shift, it requires time, patience, risk-taking, and collaboration. However, it also holds the potential to redefine learning experiences for children and adults in the process of connecting, wondering, playing, and discovering together.

Extended Learning Experiences

Digital learning portfolios provide a variety of options for communicating with families. These platforms present students with opportunities for engaging in their learning by demonstrating, documenting, and sharing with teachers and families. Offering students new levels of ownership for their work through technology allows them to capture individual learning experiences that are reflective of their specific growth and development.

Our Digital Portfolio Selection

There are many digital portfolio platforms to choose from! As you have learned from previous chapters, we appreciate the space that Seesaw provides for student, teacher, and family communication. Extended Learning Experiences are posted in student journals on Seesaw. You will come to learn how we use Google Sites as another platform to communicate learning stories to families. When a new page is added to the site, the published link is posted in Seesaw to students' journals.

In addition to students creating, educators also have the unique opportunity to create and tell the stories of learning happening in the classroom. **Extended Learning Experiences are multimedia learning stories that are woven together using a variety of sources such as student work samples, documentation of the process of learning, and resources to support conversation and discovery beyond the classroom.** They can be shared within the digital portfolio and are meant to guide families in gaining a deeper understanding of the context for their child's learning by creating a window into the educational experience as a whole.

Innovating Play Bonus Resources: Find more at
innovatingplay.world/kindergartentour
innovatingplay.world/inspirationalstart
innovatingplay.world/frontloadingconnections
innovatingplay.world/offeringresources

Learning stories are inclusive of all families as they often transcend language, written word, and cultural differences by focusing on the feel of learning through photos, videos, songs, and safe interactions between home and school. In this chapter we break down and share examples of Extended Learning Experiences as spaces for development of anticipatory sets, culmination of experiences, and communication of special projects.

Anticipatory Sets

An anticipatory set is a short activity given at the very beginning of a lesson to get students' attention, activate prior knowledge, and prepare them for learning. It plays a key role for educators, as it provides the "hook" for student engagement in the learning that is about to take place. While this is traditionally done as part of a classroom lesson, we have discovered that there are wonderful advantages to including families in this part of the process. These types of Extended Learning Experiences hold the potential to level the playing field as they guide families through meaningful discussion and create common connections before learning takes place in the classroom. They may be shared the day or week prior, or over the weekend, in order to allow the family ample time to experience this part of the learning process together.

Before the School Year Begins

Even before students enter our classrooms, we can begin to create a sense of safety and purpose for our learning together. We reach out to our families prior to the start of the school year and invite them to connect with students' digital learning portfolios right away. For us, this means offering access to students' individual Seesaw accounts. When families set up their account and check their child's learning portfolio for the first time, they are intentionally greeted with two Extended Learning Experiences in the form of videos. The first video is a short tour through the classroom, answering the common questions students might have when starting the school year. Having a sense of simple routines and classroom spaces offers families guidance in having meaningful conversations, which may ease worries about the year ahead.

A TOUR OF KINDERGARTEN

What will I do with all of my things?

Still images were uploaded to Adobe Spark. Voice narration, question text, and music were also added through the tool.

In addition to helping them feel safe, we like to offer families a video to enjoy together that will inspire and excite them. Creating a short movie trailer using photos from the prior year can capture that feeling in a way that reaches adults and children alike. When families are greeted with a glimpse into the classroom that addresses curiosity and excitement, we take an important step toward firmly establishing the expectation that they will be participating in collaboration and partnership opportunities between home and school.

AN INSPIRATIONAL START

Still images of children and the classroom environment and snippets of video from Seesaw recordings were imported into iMovie. Transition text and music were added using the program's tools.

Signs of Spring

In this example, we explore the potential for learning by offering families simple visual guidance to help them engage in conversation about the surrounding world with their child before learning takes place in the classroom. As we were preparing to learn about signs of spring as part of our literacy and science curriculum, we wanted to highlight observations of current changes in nature. To get children ready to think about the connection between weather, environment, and seasons, we shared a movie trailer with a variety of photos representing seasonal shifts. The movie trailer not only prepares children for upcoming content, but also captures a feel for learning. Through a simple one-minute video, we can stimulate meaningful conversation between family members. We can also start to encourage children to closely observe the things that are happening in their world outside the classroom.

The storyboard layout was used in iMovie to import pictures from the website PhotosForClass.com.

Building Knowledge with Families

As educators we have the responsibility to guide students in developing a rich and meaningful knowledge base. This means that ultimately, learning should connect to real experiences, curiosities, observations, and discoveries about the world. The following example is an Extended Learning Experience that is shared once a unit of study has begun in the classroom, but which has the potential to move beyond the classroom through family participation.

An Adobe Spark Page opens up a variety of opportunities for families to experience learning together. As an alternative to homework, we can offer access to resources that have been used during lessons. Families are given access to visual images and questions for discussion at home. Videos, songs, and poems provide opportunities for revisiting familiar text and oral language that are key for reading development, especially in young children. In this space we can also provide examples of cross-curricular experiences so that families can revisit connections with children at home. This is a wonderful opportunity to invite families to participate by sharing photos or videos from home, allowing for the continuous flow of learning between home and school.

OFFERING RESOURCES

Look at the photos below with your child. Talk about the following questions together:

1. How are the pictures the same? How are they different?
2. What kind of tree do you think the different leaves came from? How do you know?
3. Name the different colors that you see. What do the colors tell you about the leaf? What do the colors tell you about the season?

Images, videos, and buttons that can lead to more resources were easily inserted into an Adobe Spark Page. After publishing, we shared a link with families via Seesaw.

Culminating Experience

When preparing to bring closure to a learning experience, we have the opportunity to merge the learning process with discoveries in order to solidify understanding and share beyond the walls of the classroom. As we develop experiences from beginning to end, we recognize the continuous art of balancing tech and hands-on experiences for very specific purposes. Engaging in physical experiences allows children to solidify their understanding by activating the connection between their brains and bodies as learners.

Marrying the tech with the hands-on approach creates potential to increase students' depth of knowledge as we capture learning in visual and auditory formats. Through Extended Learning Experiences focusing on culmination, students are given additional ways of processing learning, including new conversations that allow them to reflect upon the experience with their families.

Retelling of Mrs. Wishy-Washy

In this example, we reflect on balancing hands-on and tech experiences as we explored learning through Playing at the Farm. As we develop and guide experiences for our students, we are open to finding a variety of ways to naturally and continuously flow from digital modes to hands-on modes and back again.

After students had created their animal drawings for the farm project, we used their work in multiple ways. As shared in Chapter 5, we used the drawings to create the digital mural for collaborative exploration of animal facts. After being added to the mural, drawings were then laminated to create felt board pieces for storytelling.

Innovating Play Bonus Resources:
Find more at innovatingplay.world/artplay

This play-based literacy experience provided a perfect opportunity to connect a new Extended Reading Experience with the fiction text *Mrs. Wishy-Washy* by Joy Cowley. After exploring the focus text throughout the following week, students used the storytelling pieces along with Adobe Spark to create a digital retelling of the story. This was shared with families via Seesaw and made available in the reading corner of the classroom for students to both view and practice retelling the story using the felt board pieces.

PLAYING WITH ART IN PHYSICAL AND DIGITAL SPACES

Children's drawings were cut out and laminated to
manipulate on a felt board.

ChatterPix allowed students to draw a mouth on their animal
and make it retell a part of *Mrs. Wishy-Washy*.

The ChatterPix video was imported into Adobe Spark Video,
which offered the ability to add text, voice narrations, and
images to retell the story.

Snowy Sight Words in Book Creator

Having an authentic audience connected to the process and the published product of a culminating experience can provide new levels of engagement for students. In this example, students were given the opportunity to share their work with families and to create a learning center that would be enjoyed by friends in their classroom in New Jersey, as well as the children in California.

> **Innovating Play Bonus Resources:** Find more at innovatingplay.world/reviewandteach

In Chapter 4 we shared the Extended Reading Experience focused on the Invitation to Play in the Snow. During that project, we offered a variety of extensions to support learning. One of those extensions began by inviting children to practice sight words using trays of salt, silver glitter, and small snowflake confetti. Snowball cards with sight words written on them provided references for the words they were meant to practice. This multi-sensory approach supports rich learning, as it connects a tactile experience with visual memory for words. We then recorded videos of children writing, spelling, and reading each word, which added accountability for completing the task and purpose for learning.

To create the culminating piece of work that would be shared with multiple audiences, a word video from each child was uploaded into Book Creator. Students worked individually with the teacher using the text and audio features in Book Creator to add a corresponding sentence to each page. When the experience was complete, the link to the published book was shared with families through Seesaw so that children could practice sight words at home. The published book was then used in both New Jersey and California kindergarten classrooms, as children could view the published book on Chromebooks and iPads while practicing words in the snow trays as they were guided by their peers.

CREATING TO REVIEW AND TEACH OTHERS

New Jersey children created a sight word in a snowy sand tray. The spelling and reading of the word was captured in a Seesaw video, which the teacher downloaded and then uploaded into Book Creator. The resource was shared with families and friends in both classes.

Exploring Goldy

School days are filled with a variety of rich learning experiences from beginning to end. We have found that Google Slides is a wonderful tool for organizing the flow of instruction and moving learning beyond the classroom. An example of using slides in this way was presented in Chapter 4 when we gave you a walk-through of Extended Reading at home with "Pat-a-Cake."

In this culminating experience example, we delve deeper into exploring this idea. During our literacy block, we used an emergent reader text based on the story of "Goldilocks and the Three Bears." To build this experience, we compiled a selection of Morning Messages, videos, songs, visual reading strategies, games, and projects that were organized in the slide deck for classroom instruction during the week.

To create a meaningful culminating experience at the end of the

Innovating Play Bonus Resources:
Find more at innovatingplay.world/goldyshare

week, select slides were moved over to a new slide deck that would be shared with families. Adding captions to the slides in this new space helped to redefine the experience for families who would view and participate in it. Additions to the slides included the rationale for learning, as well as guiding questions for families. Game directions, photos of games in progress, and slides for playing the game at home were all included as well. Finally, seeing photos of the process of group work along with final products that live in the classroom allowed families to see the learning that had taken place over the course of the week.

Instead of creating a brand-new Extended Learning Experience, consider what you have already created for students in Google Slides and bring it to the next level as a culminating piece to share with families!

USING FACILITATION SLIDES FOR FAMILY SHARING

Exploring Goldy

Bringing Our Learning Home

Click through the slides to see our learning in action and find ways to extend experiences at home!

What do we know about sentences?

We worked together to build sentences from our focus text.

Teams worked together to unscramble the words and build their sentence.

Check out our sentences and illustrations!

Inviting families to see the learning happening in the classroom and to participate in the process has the potential to redefine the educational experience. One of the key elements in this shift is the creation of a space in which family participation is represented, acknowledged, and celebrated as part of a larger learning community. We propose that using Extended Learning Experiences as a new approach to "home" work offers a valuable contribution to learning through the collective and meaningful transfer of knowledge beyond the walls of the classroom.

A true Extended Learning Experience takes learning a step further by supporting caregivers through modeling and guidance, while giving them space to grow, learn, and contribute. Rather than being an isolated practice, which is often presented through conventional homework, this approach is both reflective and reciprocal. Families are no longer outside viewers and consumers of their child's learning experience. Instead, caregivers are invited to make active contributions to the learning community alongside their child. Through each experience we cultivate, we encourage all participants to develop and grow toward becoming effective and positive communicators living in a digital culture.

Using a Class Website as a Multidimensional Tool

Creating a website is often a district requirement for educators. Teachers of older students may focus on clear communication and development of spaces that directly support effective learning. Those who work with younger children have a different type of process and audience to consider. Early childhood educators often approach the creation of a website strictly as a source of communication from school to home. We invite you to consider the possibilities in building a space that will nurture, expand, and include families in the learning process. In this section we provide three examples of pages from our shared class website.

Innovating Play Bonus Resources: Find more at sites.google.com/view/canj1819sharing/home

As we began to discover the amazing learning that was unfolding between our classes, we quickly saw the need for a space to capture it all. We wanted to offer families in both places a cohesive and consistent space to which they could return in order to experience the journey with us. We also saw the value in working collaboratively to develop the space together. Creating a beautiful and meaningful website is a significant task to undertake along with facilitating classroom learning each day.

Our Platform Selection for a Shared Family Site

There are a variety of platforms you can use to make a class website. We needed a tool that would allow us both to contribute to the site. We also wanted an option that would allow us to work collaboratively at the same time. These were some of the reasons we chose to create our shared website in Google Sites. Another factor was the fact that we use a lot of Google Apps, all of which embed nicely within Google Sites.

As classroom teachers participating in a daily cross-country collaboration, we considered workflow and efficiency in each process along the way. Working smarter to create a shared site would mean that we could each contribute our individual talents to the creation, which would benefit all of our families.

From the beginning of development, we set the intention that our site would provide a big-picture look at the learning on both sides of the country. This would be a dedicated space to capture our classes' processes and discoveries, while offering families opportunities to expand exploration beyond the classroom.

When we considered teacher intentions for a website, we asked ourselves:

- How can we develop a story of learning that can be shared and revisited individually by children and collectively by families?
- How can we capture the process and products of learning through multiple tools and formats in one consistent space?

- How can we create a meaningful space that provides scaffolding and practical guidance for families as partners in learning?

A class website is a blank canvas for storytelling of all kinds. As teachers of young children we have the opportunity to weave together learning stories that allow students to reflect upon experiences while including families in learning alongside us. In this example, we share how we bring families into the daily learning that takes place between our classrooms over the course of the year.

Innovating Play Bonus Resources: Find more at sites.google.com/view/canj1819sharing/ environmental-print-chat sites.google.com/view/canj1819sharing/ reading-strategies

Throughout Part 1 of this book we introduced a variety of routines and rituals that are shared between classes on a daily basis. As we establish these daily routines with children in the classroom, we give families access to their ongoing development through our shared site. The home page includes photos, videos, and embedded elements displaying our daily routines and rituals. When children are transitioning into the school year, the site can provide a source of comfort by offering a common language between school and home. As the school year progresses, families can help children process their growth and reflect on changes over time.

Throughout any given week there are a variety of experiences happening in the classroom. As educators we have the privilege of participating in this process with our students each day. As we look for strategies to deepen learning, we consider the potential of visually documenting learning in a consistent space. Many of the experiences shared in this book were shared with families through our shared site.

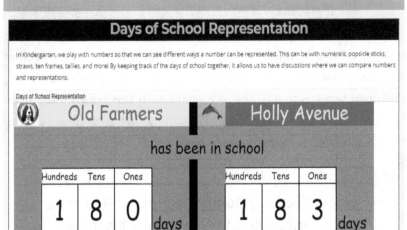

SHARING THE DIGITAL SPACES WE USE EVERY DAY!

Days of School Representation

In Kindergarten, we play with numbers so that we can see different ways a number can be represented. This can be with numerals, popsicle sticks, straws, ten frames, tallies, and more! By keeping track of the days of school together, it allows us to have discussions where we can compare numbers and representations.

Days of School Representation

Old Farmers | Holly Avenue

has been in school

Hundreds	Tens	Ones
1	8	0

days

Hundreds	Tens	Ones
1	8	3

days

Our Days of School Representation is set up in Google Sheets. Google Apps have the ability to "publish to the web," which allows us to embed the document on a website and surface what is most recent in the document. This means whenever the website is loaded, the most recent information from that document will be updated and displayed without our having to do a thing!

If you are using Google Sites to build your website, importing Google Apps is as simple as locating a Google Doc in a Google Drive search and clicking on it to bring it into your site. (Be sure to change the sharing settings to "anyone can view.")

In the following example, we share the ways that a page on our site was used to gather the process, products, and extension experiences from our very first real-time kindergarten chat between our classes (i.e., live video chat in Google Meet). Our focus was on exploring environmental print in each of our local spaces.[1] On this page of our site we highlighted the ways that we used Morning Message, literature connections, and a song and game with students in our classrooms. We also invited all families to participate in our learning by taking photos of children alongside examples of environmental prints they had identified in the world. Once families responded with the photos, we

---

1   Environmental print is the print you can find in everyday life, such as on signs, labels, and logos.

included them on the web page for this experience. What may have otherwise stayed in the classroom, only to be experienced by those students and teachers, has become part of a collective experience that is shared within our cross-country learning community.

Witnessing the process from the classroom and ways children are learning out in the world empowers families to see how they can contribute to the ongoing development of knowledge and understanding for children. In this way, all members of the home, school, and cross-country communities have value and are able to take ownership of learning together.

As teachers we face the daily challenge of finding enough time in the day to meet the needs of each and every learner in the classroom. As much as we try to differentiate and personalize learning, all children would benefit from quiet, uninterrupted time with specific support that meets their instructional needs. While our classrooms may not always be as conducive to this type of instruction as we would like, we do have the opportunity to empower families to work with us in order to fill some of these gaps.

PIECING TOGETHER AN EXPERIENCE

To share the context and roots of exploring our environment, we included an image on our site that led to the collaborative book we made in Book Creator.

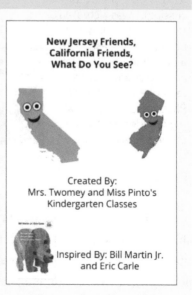

New Jersey Friends, California Friends, What Do You See?

Created By:
Mrs. Twomey and Miss Pinto's
Kindergarten Classes

Inspired By: Bill Martin Jr.
and Eric Carle

Morning Messages that were used in class on the day of our live video chat were downloaded as images from Google Slides and imported into the site.

An invitation to play (to extend the environmental print discussion) was created in Google Drawings, posted to Seesaw to invite buddies to play, and included on our site to serve as a reference. Photos from participating families were added to the page as well.

While we recognize that not every caregiver will be comfortable working with his or her child this way, we see it as our responsibility to offer families resources that open up possibilities for supporting their child. Common language and clear understanding of learning approaches and strategies help to ensure that children who receive support from caregivers outside of school will receive consistent messages.

In this example, we use the environmental print page of our website to offer families resources on reading strategies that are taught in the classroom. Visuals and videos are offered so that children and caregivers can see strategies modeled before practicing on their own. Increasing exposure, developing consistent language, and creating transparency in learning strategies and approaches deepens the respect and partnership between home and school.

Acknowledging Challenges and Moving Forward

As classroom teachers we would be remiss in writing a book for our community of readers that did not include a look at the real challenges we face when working with families. While we see the potential in this area and stand behind all of our ideas, we also know that family challenges can feel like insurmountable roadblocks in education. Teachers can become discouraged when we feel like the challenges are too big for us to even make a dent in them. As we conclude this chapter, we would like to share these thoughts with you.

In making educational decisions that have the potential to impact learning through families, we fully recognize that all we can do is offer options and provide guidance. For us this means taking a deep breath and guiding families through a process of nurturing. We approach families with the same caring, understanding, and support that we show our students each day. We acknowledge that each family is facing their own dynamics, challenges, and daily struggles. However we would like to share some thoughts with every teacher who has read this chapter and sees these Extended Learning Experiences as being beyond the realm of what is possible in their classroom.

For every family that an Extended Learning Experience may fail to reach, let's consider the families it *does* reach. Let's take time to contemplate the overwhelmed and exhausted caregiver who sees an inspirational video reflecting his child's learning over the past week. This two-minute visual experience can spark a conversation with his or her child that may not have happened before. Connection and shared curiosity support the child in solidifying learning, while the caregiver finds new energy and value as a participant in his child's education.

Now let's think about the child who chooses to scroll through her learning portfolio in the classroom and clicks on an Extended Learning Experience to relive and process her learning. She is given the opportunity to develop deeper connections, because she has access to a space that represents her learning as a complete and valuable story. These moments provide us glimmers of hope. This is the gentle shift in connection that can take place because we have opened up learning experiences in a new way.

When we change how an individual or a family views learning, feels about school, or experiences the world, we create a potential ripple. As we approach any Extended Learning Experience, we focus our energy and intention on the shifts and ripples that we may create for families who have access to our learning stories. Whether children and caregivers quietly view experiences or jump in with contributions, we provide new possibilities for developing the learning experience and participating in the community together. Extended Learning Experiences offer families and teachers hope. Beyond this, they offer action that puts hope into motion. This is all any of us can do as we attempt to change the world and nurture each other.

Concluding Thoughts

As you take in the Innovating Play Cycle and prepare to discover, refine, or reflect on your work as an educator, we have some final thoughts for you to consider. For every beautifully outlined experience you have just read, we offer the following gentle reminders.

The months we spent writing this book were filled with days of planning, organizing, preparing, and teaching in the classroom. There were school committee meetings, staff meetings, parent–teacher conferences, assessments, and report cards, among other teacher responsibilities that needed to be fulfilled. All of this is to say that we know the demands placed on educators. We also know how the work goes way beyond the hours of the school day in our hearts and minds. We know the life teachers are living because we are in it too. We are kindergarten teachers.

Each chapter in this book is intended to provide words, visuals, and inspiration that help you to experience life in our classrooms. It was with deep gratitude that we embraced the opportunity to write a book in which we could joyfully throw our classroom doors wide open and invite you inside. We hope that you have felt welcomed and nurtured in the process of reading.

As our classroom guests, we need you to know this important detail as well: For every perfect scene we painted in this book, real classroom life was in progress. During any one of the experiences we have shared, there may have been tears that needed to be wiped, wiggly teeth that fell out, shoes that needed to be tied, Band-Aids that needed to be applied, and potentially a dozen different stories attempting to be told at once by five- and six-year-olds who were learning to coexist in one space. As anyone who works with young children knows, sometimes this entire list of events can happen at the exact same time. We know the deep breath, the patient smile, and the need to laugh it off at the end of the day. We are kindergarten teachers.

You may have picked up this book as a fellow educator of young children wondering how to creatively integrate technology in your classroom. You may be an administrator looking to support your primary school teachers as they look for ways to continue to learn and grow. You may be a technology coach or specialist looking to bridge the worlds of technology and elementary education. Whatever your role in education, we are reminding you that for all of the technological advances that have been made, the heart of early childhood remains the same. It is our job as teachers who passionately wish to protect the natural development of their young students to patiently and lovingly take on the potentially messy, often joyful, and sometimes trying task of teaching young children the art of learning, both in our classrooms and out in the world.

As you move forward we encourage you to protect and nurture the heart of your work with young children. For every lesson you develop, whether it is hands-on learning or blended with tech, let it reflect the child's need to discover how to navigate the larger world as safely, gently, and authentically as possible. Our young students need these lessons more than ever.

Beyond the classroom, we encourage you to let your work find new ways to guide families toward seeing and feeling their role as valuable contributors to the learning experience. Together we can honor family bonds and relationships as part of the educational process. When you feel like giving up (and we know that feeling too), take a deep breath and refocus. Keep moving forward, and provide a model from which your whole community of learners can grow.

As you sit down with any piece of technology in order to plan, organize, create, or facilitate learning in ways that may push beyond the current norm, stop and wonder aloud: "Who are the people that will be nurtured through this action?" Consider ways to broaden that list of people. Be brave. Together we can embrace technology as a source of connection, depth, and possibilities that are worth exploring because they provide us with an opportunity to nurture a human, a family, a community.

Let it get messy.

Let it be authentic.

Trust that it is worth it.

Let's change the world together.

We are educators.

Learning with the #InnovatingPlay Community

How can we offer opportunities for conversation and extensions from school that bring learning home in meaningful and practical ways?

innovatingplay.world/bookq14

Share a tool that allows you to support growth and learning because of the ways in which it connects people.

innovatingplay.world/bookq15

Part
Four

Moving Forward

Connecting with a Professional Learning Network

In an attempt to empower educators to put action behind their own visions for Innovating Play, this section of the book offers a multitude of specific actions and resources to help you move forward. We offer many of the tips and tricks we have discovered along the way to support you on your journey. In addition to providing links to resources throughout the book, we are also sharing specific planning templates to support classroom practices. You can access our sample schedules to see what a day in its entirety might look like in our classrooms. As always, we invite you to make a copy and customize the templates to reflect what will work best for you and your students. Each of our shared templates may be considered an invitation to play alongside us as you embrace Innovating Play with students, families, and colleagues across the country.

Finding an Online Community

Participating in an online community of educators who embrace your mindset, values, and practices in the classroom can have a huge impact on your professional growth. A professional learning network (PLN) is a group of professionals with whom you choose to surround yourself. Having a community that goes beyond the space of your school district allows you to connect with professionals anywhere in the world. You can share wonders, play with others' ideas, offer your own innovations, and discover more about your pedagogy as an educator.

We cannot stress enough how important it is that you pause and take the time to initiate a PLN and nurture your professional self. The experiences that you have read in this book happened because we took time to place value on and pursue our professional growth *first*. We could not have written anything in this book without a strong connection to our PLN. Had we not taken the time to develop our PLNs, this book would not be in your hands today.

A perk to developing your PLN is that it is yours. This means you can decide how much time you spend connecting with others and whom you connect with. Take ownership of your PLN, and join us. Possibilities that you may never have pondered await. Your collaborating teacher could be out there waiting for you! In this section, we will use the Innovating Play model to share more about each stage of discovering your PLN.

Wondering as a Community

Perhaps one of the most important shifts in mindset for educators is the idea that teachers no longer need to be experts in everything. As educators it is our responsibility to support students in navigating how to be

Maximize Feedback Opportunities

Be sure to share your questions while using hashtags and tagging educators to receive feedback.

learners in the world. Rather than knowing all of the answers, we want to model for them how to ask questions in order to problem-solve and find solutions. In sharing our wonders, we can connect more deeply with our learning and open up opportunities for innovation.

To embrace this mindset we need to surround ourselves with others in the community who are willing to ask questions. This means that the culture of the community needs to be a safe space in which all members feel heard, validated, and supported in wondering out loud. As you build your PLN and find professionals who inspire you, we encourage you to be brave in asking questions so you can obtain the resources or knowledge that will help you grow.

Playing Together as a Community

Making the decision to become part of a community of educators from around the world means that everything you do in the classroom has the potential to impact your students *and* students beyond your space. Our Innovating Play Community is built with educators who are ready to share a spark for a new idea and then lean into feedback and support to bring it to fruition. Through discussion and thoughtful responses, teachers encourage each other to try new things and are often willing to play together. It is neat to see connections and sparks shared between teachers and coaches who work in different spaces and are ready to play! This collaboration can lend itself to enhancing your teaching craft and improve learning experiences for your students. Exploring possibilities for teachers and kids to begin playing together on a consistent basis in classrooms around the world is one of the important ways we are redefining education.

Invite Others to Play

Think: What are my students and I doing in the classroom that we can extend by working with others?

Include a photo and hashtags in your post!

Discovering as a Community

Inevitably the process of playing together leads to amazing new discoveries. Together we can celebrate new things that worked and consider alternatives or points of growth for things that may not have gone as planned. Honest discovery and growth comes from all kinds of experiences. When we share discoveries as a community, we create new points for connection. It is here that we find common ground to move forward in our work together, and we can once again begin the Innovating Play Cycle.

Share and Reflect

Celebrate what your students are doing in your classroom. This is a great opportunity for you to reflect and also allows others to discover an idea they can take to their own classrooms.

Connecting with a Collaborating Teacher

We are lucky to live in a time when educators are able to connect in a variety of ways. Social media offers wonderful platforms for finding educators who are ready to collaborate and share their ideas and resources. Twitter was our chosen space, as it offers opportunities to participate in education discussions with a range of topics and grants 24/7 access to educators around the world. While the platform was foreign at first, we soon learned how to navigate and find what we needed. Hashtags can help filter content or connect you with a specific group of people. We have a lovely tribe on the #InnovatingPlay hashtag, and we would be happy to connect with you too (@jlabar2me, @PintoBeanz11). Creating a professional Twitter space and being thoughtful about who you follow can help you develop a Twitter feed that is reflective of your mindset as an educator and provides limitless sources of inspiration. Take advantage of the "Learning with the #InnovatingPlay Community" boxes throughout this book.

Once you have embraced a community of like-minded educators, taking a step toward opening up your classroom and joining forces with a specific teacher is an empowering decision for educators and students. Before taking the leap into daily collaboration, it's important to spend time finding a fellow educator who will support you, inspire you, and be ready to take risks with you. Using our experience as a guide, we invite you to consider the following thoughts on finding a teacher for daily collaboration:

- **Choose someone who inspires you and complements your practice and mindset in the classroom.** Look for teachers who are sharing amazing practices, and start connecting with them.

- **Find someone who is open to exploring and learning and shares a similar comfort level with digital tools.** If you are both beginners, learn together! There's a good chance that you will each discover tips and tricks to share with each other along the way.

- **Be ready to play the role of mentor and student.** Teachers who work together best move fluidly between the roles of teacher and learner. Be honest about your strengths and areas where you need to grow.

- **Choose someone who makes you feel safe.** Daily collaboration means you will be spending the entire year together. Both teachers should feel comfortable sharing ideas, acting on them in the classroom, and participating in honest reflection.

- **Be ready to explore tools beyond what you use with students in the classroom.** Remember that teachers who are facilitating experiences together will also need to find spaces to collaboratively plan and reflect. Whether you try the chat features within Google Apps or other communication apps, remaining open to exploring a variety of communication platforms is essential to finding what works for both of you.

In the beginning of this book we posed the question: How can we plan and discover together as teachers? Through our years of collaborative teaching, we have facilitated and created amazing new classroom experiences. We have come to learn that our work together has redefined each of our experiences as educators. As you move forward, we encourage you to consider collaboration without limits. Find your people, and find your person. These will be the professionals who inspire you, who push you to grow, who lift you up and lean into discovery alongside you. They will be the people who remind you of your potential, who help you see and feel your magic, and who support you in helping your students find theirs. So take a leap of faith, be brave in your role as an educator, and remember how many possibilities are in the words, "Do you want to play?"

Innovating Play Bonus Resources: Find more at innovatingplay.world/collaboratingteacher

Learning with the #InnovatingPlay Community

Which hashtags and educators do you enjoy following?

innovatingplay.world/bookq16

How has your PLN impacted you as an educator?

innovatingplay.world/bookq17

Even More Resources for Innovating Play

Our Schedules

I n this section we provide a sample schedule for both of our kindergarten classrooms. A daily schedule provides a structure for focusing each day while keeping balance and consistency for instruction. While we strive to maintain the schedule on a daily basis, we also recognize the need for flexibility in the classroom. We continuously explore ways to stay true to the basic framework on any given day, while providing options for discovery through unique learning experiences.

Many of the special projects presented in this book were divided into pieces to match the classroom structure and thereby woven into the day. Rather than being seen as extra, these opportunities for deep connection can create the foundation for experiencing learning as part of the daily schedule.

Jessica's Schedule

- 8:50–9:15 Connected Play
- 9:15–9:40 Community Gathering
- 9:40–10:00 Playing with Words/Orton-Gillingham
- 10:00–10:40 Extended Reading Experience/Literacy Learning Choices
- 10:40–11:00 Creating with Words Mini-Lesson
- 11:05–11:30 Lunch
- 11:30–12:00 Recess
- 12:00–12:25 Creating with Words
- 12:25–1:05 Math
- 1:10–1:55 Specials (related arts)
- 1:55–2:05 Snack
- 2:10–2:50 Science/Community Play/STREAM/ Outdoor Classroom
- 2:50–3:00 Reflection and Goal-Setting
- 3:00–3:05 Personal Reflection/Pack Up

Christine's Schedule

- 8:20–8:45 Connected Play
- 8:45–9:20 Community Gathering
- 9:20–9:45 Playing with Words
- 9:45–10:05 Extended Reading
- 10:10–10:30 Recess
- 10:30–11:10 Creating with Words
- 11:20–12:03 Lunch
- 12:15–1:45 Math or Rotations (various subject integrations)
- 1:45–2:15 Community Play
- 2:15–2:30 Personal Reflection/Pack Up

Community Gathering—During this time we cover the Wish You Well, Feelings Check-In, and Morning Message.

Math—This block begins with counting days of school and tuning in to weather reports.

Anchor Charts for Routines

As routines are introduced, we maintain a consistent space for creating and collecting visuals to support student understanding and independence. Using an anchor chart template in Google Slides, teachers and students work together to articulate the specifics of each routine.

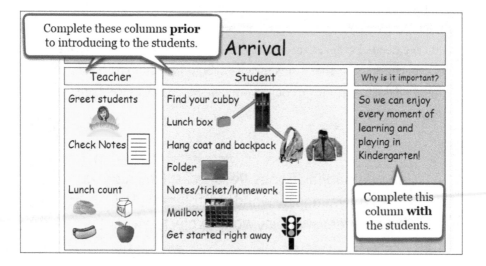

Student tasks are put in order and documented through simple words and pictures. Teacher responsibilities are also clearly outlined so that the classroom community as a whole is held accountable for contributing to the success of the routine. In addition to tasks, a third column on the chart is used to document why a routine is important for the whole community within the flow of the day.

Innovating Play Bonus Resources: Find more at
innovatingplay.world/anchortemplate
innovatingplay.world/samplecharts

A slide deck can be dedicated to developing and finalizing all of the anchor charts. It is helpful to bring specific chart slides that are used on a daily basis into a weekly slide deck that you use to facilitate the learning experiences.

Collaborative Lesson Plan

Just as it helps to have a consistent schedule, having a space for meaningful lesson planning ensures that learning experiences remain focused and productive. When we began collaborating on a daily basis, we knew that we needed a space to organize thoughts and communicate ideas when planning together. (This meant we both needed to have access to the same document so we could work collaboratively as we shared and organized ideas.)

Innovating Play Bonus Resources: Find more at innovatingplay.world/collablessonplan innovatingplay.world/projectplan

Every planning session begins by brainstorming elements that allow teachers to build a variety of play-based lessons while staying true to academic expectations. Essential questions help us to communicate the big picture and purpose for learning. Specific learning standards maintain accountability for exposure and mastery of grade-level expectations. We also include "I can" statements, which are used in play boards and Morning Messages in order to help communicate learning goals to students. Creating space for each of these elements alongside lesson activities allows us to weave together rich learning experiences throughout the week.

In our Collaborative Lesson Plan Template, you will find tables for various parts of our day that we use to help us fill in the elements and information we need to facilitate learning experiences. Descriptions are provided below to give you an idea of how we use each section.

Time of Day	
Learning Goals	**Activities**
We use this space for essential questions, standards, and "I can" statements. This helps us ensure that connections are present within the learning goals and that activities are developmentally appropriate.	In addition to activity descriptions, pictures and links are included to visually communicate what the activity looks like.
Mental Notes	
We usually use this space to communicate materials that will be used, past/future connections, and reminders of supplemental pieces that need to be collected or created.	

Lesson Plan/Thematic Approach

Use this template as a guide to planning, sparking inspiration, and creating meaningful play-based learning experiences.

Title, Theme, or Area(s) of Focus

Connect

Guiding Questions:
- What is the connecting piece, the tie, that is bringing you together?
- What concepts or ideas help kids bridge previous learning/experiences to the next set of concepts and ideas?

Learning Objectives:
What goals do the classes share that need to be worked on?

Wonder

Guiding Questions:
- How will you create wonder?
- How are you going to capture the kids' questions?

Play

Guiding Question:
- How and where will the experience(s) be facilitated?

Discover

Guiding Questions:
- How will you guide reflection?
- What tools will you use for documentation?

#InnovatingPlay #SlowFlipChat Archive

In addition to connecting on Twitter, we created and moderated a variety of discussions using a #SlowFlipChat model. In this model, questions were posted weekly on Twitter, and a Flipgrid space was available for teachers to respond in a video format. Video responses allowed for more personal connection and reflective and thoughtful discussion. The Flipgrids remain available for viewing, as they provide a wonderful selection of ideas and resources that can be used by teachers anywhere and allow for ongoing inspiration.

Innovating Play Bonus Resources:
Find more at innovatingplay.world/slowflipchat

Acknowledgments

We are extremely grateful for the support of those who have contributed to the vision behind this book. While we have had the privilege of creating and nurturing the work, so many people have played valuable roles in bringing the mindset and practices of *Innovating Play* to life. To all of the people who have connected, wondered, played, and discovered alongside us near and far, we are blessed to have you on our journey. Thank you for your contributions and your belief in limitless learning that can be shared by all. We would like to extend a special thank-you to:

- Our students and families, especially the collaborating classes of 2018, 2019, and 2020, for being ready to learn and play in new ways
- Our school districts for providing us the space to grow and explore as educators
- The #InnovatingPlay Community for contributing their thoughts in our chats and discussions
- Our families and friends for believing in us
- Creators and companies that have developed tools to support meaningful work with technology and young children
- Our editing, designing, and publishing teams who provided the guidance, structure, and details needed to bring our vision to life

About the Authors

Christine Pinto and **Jessica LaBar-Twomey** have been in the field of early childhood education for more than twenty years collectively. Their kindergarten classes have collaborated on a daily, yearlong basis from their locations in California and New Jersey for a number of years. Christine and Jessica moderated the #InnovatingPlay/#GAfE4Littles Slow Flip Chat via Flipgrid for a year and a half and are proud to be published with Dave Burgess Consulting, Inc. When opportunities arise, Christine and Jessica travel to present about Innovating Play and how they preserve, protect, and transform early childhood experiences in and beyond the classroom.

Speaking

When speaking engagements arise and our schedules permit, we enjoy traveling to share the Innovating Play Cycle with educators. Our presenting page on innovatingplay.world has the most current listings of sessions and topics. Please email info@innovatingplay.world if you are interested in having us share at your school, district, or event.

More from

DAVE BURGESS Consulting, Inc.

Since 2012, DBCI has been publishing books that inspire and equip educators to be their best. For more information on our titles or to purchase bulk orders for your school, district, or book study, visit DaveBurgessConsulting.com/DBCIbooks.

More Teaching Methods & Materials

All 4s and 5s by Andrew Sharos

Boredom Busters by Katie Powell

The Classroom Chef by John Stevens and Matt Vaudrey

The Collaborative Classroom by Trevor Muir

Copyrighteous by Diana Gill

CREATE by Bethany J. Petty

Ditch That Homework by Matt Miller and Alice Keeler

Ditch That Textbook by Matt Miller

Don't Ditch That Tech by Matt Miller, Nate Ridgway, and Angelia Ridgway

EDrenaline Rush by John Meehan

Educated by Design by Michael Cohen, The Tech Rabbi

The EduProtocol Field Guide by Marlena Hebern and Jon Corippo

The EduProtocol Field Guide: Book 2 by Marlena Hebern and Jon Corippo

Instant Relevance by Denis Sheeran

LAUNCH by John Spencer and A.J. Juliani

Make Learning MAGICAL by Tisha Richmond

Pure Genius by Don Wettrick

The Revolution by Darren Ellwein and Derek McCoy

Shift This! by Joy Kirr

Skyrocket Your Teacher Coaching by Michael Cary Sonbert

Spark Learning by Ramsey Musallam

Sparks in the Dark by Travis Crowder and Todd Nesloney

Table Talk Math by John Stevens

The Wild Card by Hope and Wade King

The Writing on the Classroom Wall by Steve Wyborney

Like a PIRATE™ Series

Teach Like a PIRATE by Dave Burgess

eXPlore Like a Pirate by Michael Matera

Learn Like a Pirate by Paul Solarz

Play Like a Pirate by Quinn Rollins

Run Like a Pirate by Adam Welcome

Tech Like a PIRATE by Matt Miller

Lead Like a PIRATE™ Series

Lead Like a PIRATE by Shelley Burgess and Beth Houf

Balance Like a Pirate by Jessica Cabeen, Jessica Johnson, and Sarah Johnson

Lead beyond Your Title by Nili Bartley

Lead with Appreciation by Amber Teamann and Melinda Miller

Lead with Culture by Jay Billy

Lead with Instructional Rounds by Vicki Wilson

Lead with Literacy by Mandy Ellis

Leadership & School Culture

Culturize by Jimmy Casas

Escaping the School Leader's Dunk Tank by Rebecca Coda and Rick Jetter

Fight Song by Kim Bearden

From Teacher to Leader by Starr Sackstein

If the Dance Floor Is Empty, Change the Song by Joe Clark

The Innovator's Mindset by George Couros

It's OK to Say "They" by Christy Whittlesey

Kids Deserve It! by Todd Nesloney and Adam Welcome

Let Them Speak by Rebecca Coda and Rick Jetter

The Limitless School by Abe Hege and Adam Dovico

Live Your Excellence by Jimmy Casas

Next-Level Teaching by Jonathan Alsheimer

The Pepper Effect by Sean Gaillard

The Principled Principal by Jeffrey Zoul and Anthony McConnell

Relentless by Hamish Brewer

The Secret Solution by Todd Whitaker, Sam Miller, and Ryan Donlan

Start. Right. Now. by Todd Whitaker, Jeffrey Zoul, and Jimmy Casas

Stop. Right. Now. by Jimmy Casas and Jeffrey Zoul

Teachers Deserve It by Rae Hughart and Adam Welcome

Teach Your Class Off by CJ Reynolds

They Call Me "Mr. De" by Frank DeAngelis

Thrive through the Five by Jill M. Siler

Unmapped Potential by Julie Hasson and Missy Lennard

When Kids Lead by Todd Nesloney and Adam Dovico

Word Shift by Joy Kirr

Your School Rocks by Ryan McLane and Eric Lowe

Technology & Tools

50 Things You Can Do with Google Classroom by Alice Keeler and Libbi Miller

50 Things to Go Further with Google Classroom by Alice Keeler and Libbi Miller

140 Twitter Tips for Educators by Brad Currie, Billy Krakower, and Scott Rocco

Block Breaker by Brian Aspinall

Code Breaker by Brian Aspinall

Control Alt Achieve by Eric Curts

Google Apps for Littles by Christine Pinto and Alice Keeler

Master the Media by Julie Smith

Reality Bytes by Christine Lion-Bailey, Jesse Lubinsky, and Micah Shippee, PhD

Sail the 7 Cs with Microsoft Education by Becky Keene and Kathi Kersznowski

Shake Up Learning by Kasey Bell

Social LEADia by Jennifer Casa-Todd

Stepping Up to Google Classroom by Alice Keeler and Kimberly Mattina

Teaching Math with Google Apps by Alice Keeler and Diana Herrington

Teachingland by Amanda Fox and Mary Ellen Weeks

Inspiration, Professional Growth & Personal Development

Be REAL by Tara Martin

Be the One for Kids by Ryan Sheehy

The Coach ADVenture by Amy Illingworth

Creatively Productive by Lisa Johnson

Educational Eye Exam by Alicia Ray

The EduNinja Mindset by Jennifer Burdis

Empower Our Girls by Lynmara Colón and Adam Welcome

Finding Lifelines by Andrew Grieve and Andrew Sharos

The Four O'Clock Faculty by Rich Czyz

How Much Water Do We Have? by Pete and Kris Nunweiler

P Is for Pirate by Dave and Shelley Burgess

A Passion for Kindness by Tamara Letter

The Path to Serendipity by Allyson Apsey

Sanctuaries by Dan Tricarico

The SECRET SAUCE by Rich Czyz

Shattering the Perfect Teacher Myth by Aaron Hogan

Stories from Webb by Todd Nesloney

Talk to Me by Kim Bearden

Teach Better by Chad Ostrowski, Tiffany Ott, Rae Hughart, and Jeff Gargas

Teach Me, Teacher by Jacob Chastain

Teach, Play, Learn! by Adam Peterson

The Teachers of Oz by Herbie Raad and Nathan Lang-Raad

TeamMakers by Laura Robb and Evan Robb

Through the Lens of Serendipity by Allyson Apsey

The Zen Teacher by Dan Tricarico

Children's Books

Beyond Us by Aaron Polansky

Cannonball In by Tara Martin

Dolphins in Trees by Aaron Polansky

I Want to Be a Lot by Ashley Savage

The Princes of Serendip by Allyson Apsey

The Wild Card Kids by Hope and Wade King

Zom-Be a Design Thinker by Amanda Fox